# BOOK PRODUCTION GUIDE

FIFTH EDITION

# ANNA FAKTOROVICH, Ph.D.

ANAPHORA LITERARY PRESS

BROWNSVILLE, TEXAS

KatMary

ANAPHORA LITERARY PRESS
1898 Athens St.
Brownsville, TX 78520
https://anaphoraliterary.com


Book design by Anna Faktorovich, Ph.D.

Published in 2017 by Anaphora Literary Press

*Anaphora*

Book Production Guide
Anna Faktorovich—5th edition.

Library of Congress Control Number: 2012907287

**Library Cataloging Information**
Faktorovich, Anna, 1981-, author.
    Book Production Guide / Anna Faktorovich
    122 p. ; 9 in.
    ISBN-13: 978-1-937536-25-1 (softcover : alk. paper)
    ISBN-10: 1-937536-25-4
Reference / Handbooks & Manuals.
NC997-1003: Commercial Art; Advertising Art
070 News Media, Journalism & Publishing

# BOOK PRODUCTION GUIDE

_____

ANNA FAKTOROVICH

# TABLE OF CONTENTS

*#1 Rule: Speedy Production Is Better Than Endless Procrastination*

*#2 Rule: Make Sure That Those Who Buy the Book Are Happy with the Product*

# INTRODUCTION

This guide explains all of the steps involved in creating a book with the Anaphora Literary Press. It can be used by publishing industry professionals who are working for other publishing houses, want to start their own press or want to self-publish their book. This book can be a great tool in editing, marketing and design college classes.

The publishing industry is undergoing radical changes today. The major difference is the explosion in self-publishing and independent book publishing projects. These ventures are far more realistic today because of the availability and accessibility of print-on-demand printers like CreateSpace (subsidiary of Amazon), Lulu and Lightning Source (subsidiary of Ingram). Only two centuries ago, William Blake was among a string of the top poets in the British Isles after publishing runs of as few as a dozen copies. The relative price of books is much smaller today and it's not only the wealthy writer that can sell a small print run. If writers can effectively market themselves on a small scale, they make it profitable for small presses to help them reach a reading market. Larger publishing houses and traditional printers cannot afford to print runs under 500 copies, so these smaller projects can only be processed through the POD printers.

There have been several incredibly successful self-published books. One of the most notable examples is the *Elements of Style* by William Strunk and his student E. B. White, who published it for Dr. Strunk's Cornell classes. For those who are familiar with this book, it clearly does not read like a standard grammar book, diving into style elements that only a top grammarian professor knows are essential for an aspiring editor, studying English at an Ivy League school. A publisher might have asked Strunk to make it "more accessible" for a "general audience," which would have meant deleting the things that make this book unique and desirable for English students. Strunk's book now sells at least 300,000 copies per year. Even Stephen King has tried selling one of his books as a chapter-by-chapter ebook (though perhaps with less success than Strunk).

While some guides talk about editing, marketing, design and the business side of the publishing industry separately, I believe these fields are intricately linked and can best be understood side-by-side. Therefore, this book will take you through the print-on-demand publishing process in a chronological order, from the point of manuscript submission, to press releases and finally to the options for taking the book out of print at the end of a book's cycle.

Anaphora Literary Press is actively looking for authors, interns and other collaborators, so send an e-mail to director@anaphoraliterary.com, if you are interested in working with Anaphora. Submission guidelines are described on the Anaphora website at, https://anaphoraliterary.com.

# STEP 1: FINDING WRITERS

You are ready to begin your publishing business. You have familiarized yourself with the content of this book, and otherwise trained yourself in book review, editing, design and marketing. You have decided to invest time and money into the project. Now, all you need is somebody to publish. How can a new press find writers to publish? And if you are an author, what are some of the best places to find publishers that are actively soliciting writers? This section offers a list of ideas for you to consider.

## Writer's Market

*Website*: www.writersmarket.com
*Note*: Published annually in print, and listings are regularly updated online. This is one of the most popularly used resources by professional writers.

## UPenn CFP

*Website*: http://call-for-papers.sas.upenn.edu/
*Note*: One of the most popular sites for posting calls for academic papers, essays, and book chapter contributions.

## Duotrope

*Website*: https://duotrope.com/
*Note*: One of the most popular sites for short-fiction and poetry writers. There are also listings for publishers that publish chapbooks, and larger print and electronic books.

## Poets & Writers

*Website*: www.pw.org
*Note*: Has a classified section that allows for manuscripts calls.

## NewPages.com

*Website*: www.newpages.com
*Note*: Hosts a calls for submissions section, also includes a list of independent publishers.

## The Writer Magazine

*Website*:
http://writermag.com
*Note*: Allows submission of calls for manuscripts. Writers must subscribe to view the listings.

## Writer Gazette

*Website*:
http://www.writergazette.com/view-call-for-submissions
*Note*: Allows calls for submissions, which can be general or categorized by genre.

# STEP 2: MANUSCRIPT REVIEW

A typical publishing house Editor's e-mail box is likely to have dozens of daily new manuscript submissions. If you are planning on working as a professional editor, you should be prepared to see a few different categories of submissions.

The ideal submission will be the full packet. It is likely to include (depending on a particular publisher's requirements): the completed manuscript, the biography of the author, a summary or a synopsis of the book and a marketing plan. Academic publishers require a thicker submission packet, and some publishers prefer to see only sample chapters in the initial review. Reading the publisher's individual preferences is essential for selling your project.

The second large group of submissions are usually lacking key ingredients, and the Editor has to e-mail the writer, asking for the missing materials.

The third group is extremely poorly written submissions or those that clearly do not fit the publisher's current needs. To these the Editor can send prompt rejection letters. The "promptness" of the reply depends on the Editor's schedule.

The fourth group is submissions that offer interesting services, such as art or photographs, or services, or collaborative efforts. There might also be several submissions of shorter pieces for a journal or magazine the press publishes, rather than book-length submissions. These have to be addressed in a manner that fits the current needs of the press.

The manuscripts that fit the basic requirements of the press are forwarded onto Step 2 of the pre-production process: proofreading and editing. The major problems that might prevent a manuscript from moving forward are: grammar, spelling, nonsensical babbling, improper use of quotations/ citations, and poor research methods in academic books. In general, a book that appears to be poorly written, or that clearly uses fluffy prose, as opposed to a dense text is likely to be discarded. Try scanning the first 10 pages of your book (if you are submitting one for publication). If you notice numerous name and pronoun repetitions, very short words, and a general lack of concrete descriptions—you should probably spend more time on perfecting your craft before re-submitting it to publishers.

If a book passes the Editor's initial review, the Editor is likely to forward it for a closer evaluation to a reviewer (if the press has a staff of interns, or assistance for this task). The steps that should be taken at this second step in the pre-production process will be discussed in the next chapter.

# STEP 3: PROOFREADING AND EDITING

## Microsoft Word Editing Functions

The tools that proofreaders and editors use to correct a manuscript vary. The standard tool that I recommend is Microsoft Word track-changes and comments option. It will be covered briefly here. Here are the steps you should take upon opening a file that's ready for proofreading or editing.

1. Click on the "Review" Tab in Word.

2. Click on "Track Changes." The track-changes button should now be yellow, if when you do not have the mouse over it.

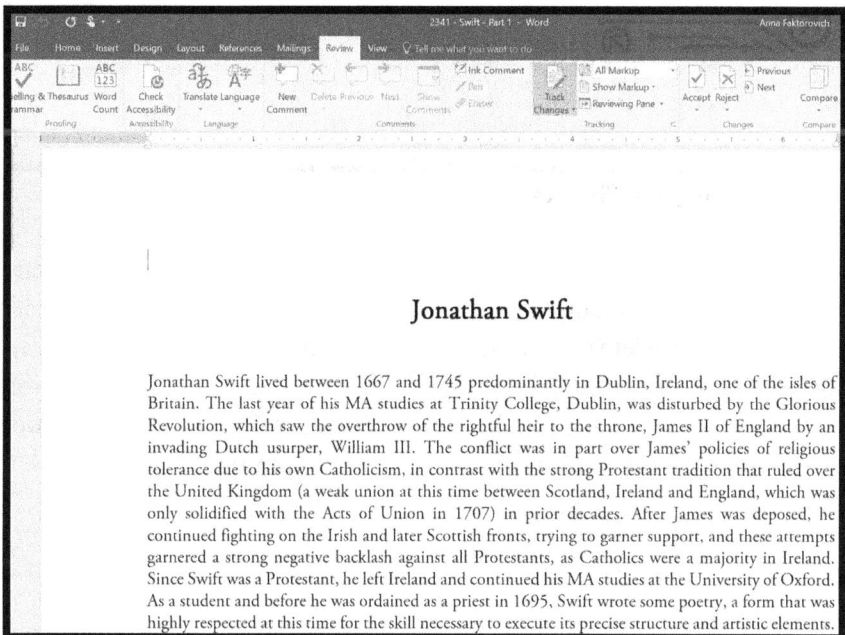

Fig. 3.1. Word Review Tab

3. Now if you add letters or words they will be typed in red, and will be underlined. If you delete letters or words out, they will be typed in red and will be crossed out. You can also click on the "Comment" option to add comments in the margins of the page. Use comments sparingly, on points that must be corrected.

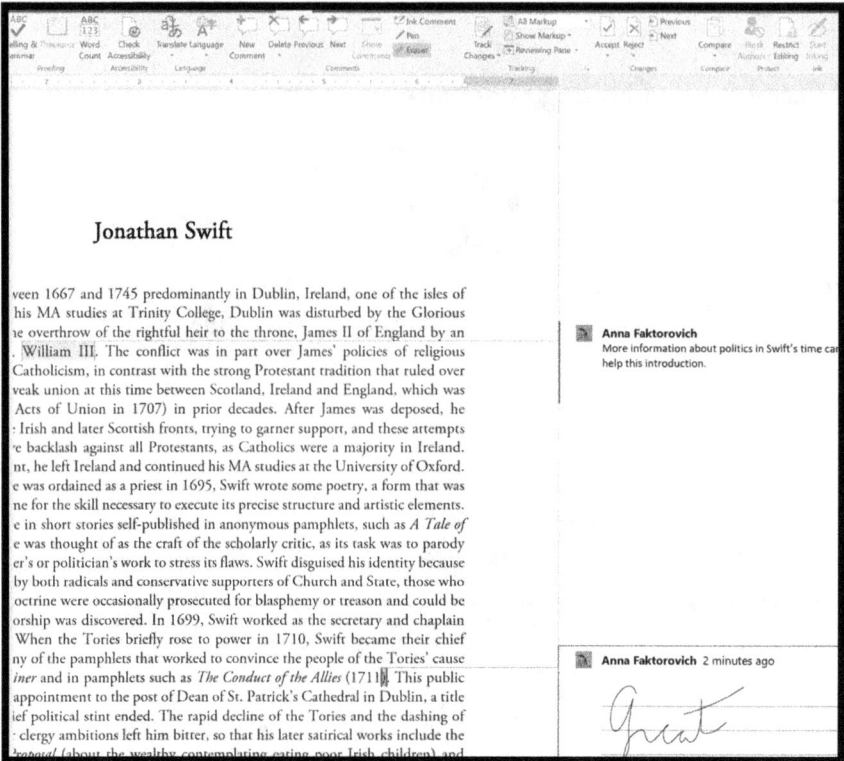

**Fig. 3.2. Word Track-Changes**

If you leave only a few marginal comments, the Editor or writer can just turn off track-changes, by clicking on the button once again, and then manually delete the comments you've left and the file will be ready for formatting and design. Of course, if you notice that there are major changes the writer has to make, or repeating errors, leaving comments on these problems is an important step in preparing a manuscript for publication.

## General Editing Advice

Proofreaders should keep in mind that the Editor might not be reviewing all of your edits after you make them. The writer, on the other hand, is likely to review all changes very closely, and is likely to complain if any mistakes are made in the editing process. Therefore, proofreaders should typically try to only change things that need to be changed, and they should re-read sentences after editing them. Thus, manuscripts that need a very thorough proofreading to be ready for publication should be rejected at the review stage, to avoid the likelihood of glitches due to miscommunication between the proofreader and the writer.

A proofreader should keep in mind that it is always useful and helpful for them to make corrections of typos, grammatical and spelling errors and of all other obvious problems. It is a good idea to have a book like *Elements of Style* on your shelf, or to double-check a grammar book or a dictionary, if you aren't sure about a grammatical change. Some grammatical glitches might be debatable, as are errors or stylistic differences, and you should be aware of these distinctions.

Here are a few common grammatical stylistic differences that are frequently mistaken for errors:

*Don't add commas after "And" or "But" at beginning of sentence.*

*Don't add or subtract commas before and—these are optional.*

Be alert to the fact that there are some unusual capitalization exceptions when you change the capitalization of a word that seems to be illogically capitalized. For example, "Bildungsroman" is capitalized—you should look up in a dictionary/ thesaurus literary terms and other words you are not familiar with to check their proper capitalization/ usage, before making changes.

You can never be sure about the spelling of words in Scots, in older versions of English, and in other linguistic variations. Here's one example: "The King's Juant." Do you know what Juant is or is referring to? So, avoid fixing these types of spellings unless you've looked up the regional/ time spelling, the word used in the original document, or you are familiar with this dialect. Definitely don't correct potentially intentional misspellings inside of quotations.

Please research the details of the rules of italics, which are pretty specific. For example, when it's a name of a series of novels "Waverley novels" isn't italicized, but the first novel in the series, by itself is italicized, *Waverley*.

Know the difference between when "the" versus "a" are used. If you notice that you keep noticing what you think is an error in the/a usage, look it up to double-check if the author had a reason to use the other variation. For example, "by the Bailie and Andrew." While it seems like "the" should be deleted in this example, the original novel uses "the Bailie" because his name is not Bailie—he is THE Bailie, or a keeper of the jail. Also, in "the *Tale*," "the" is necessary to specify that it's *the* book, otherwise the reader might think, if reading quickly that it's another "a Tale." Linguists and grammarians disagree about some of these variations—so your goal as an editor is to avoid editing these questionable points and to fix clear and necessary mistakes, of which there are usually plenty in even the best books.

*Know the basic rules of grammar and don't insert grammatical errors just to fix clarity or other problems that seem to be present:*

For example, don't separate thoughts with commas; in other words don't break the subject from the verb with a comma between them, etc.

When referring to events literature, the present tense, rather than the past tense is usually used.

## Editing Technique

Don't change text inside of quotations without adding [] around the change or inserting **...** where you make a deletion. Don't insert both [] and an ellipse, as the ellipse alone signifies that something was omitted.

Avoid deleting important bits of information—re-read sentences if you make several corrections.

"But," "however," and other direction changers shouldn't be altered so that the meaning of the sentence changes.

Don't reverse sentences or don't move large parts of the sentence from one end to the other, unless the style or grammar is significantly improved by the reversal.

## Some Common Mistakes

. . . (or three periods with spaces between them) should be changed to ... (or three periods next to each other, or into a mid-line ellipsis). It's a good idea to use the "Replace" function in Word, rather than doing these manually. But, be aware, that some writers insert a 4th period . . . . or . . ..—you want to double-check the type of . . . that the writer commonly uses and insert this into the "Replace" function, putting ... into the "Replace to" box. The replace function can also be used to delete all tabs in a word document, replacing them with automatic line indentations, to avoid having inconsistent indentations across a given document.

To use the "Replace" function in Word:

1. Go to the "Home" tab.

2. Click on the "Replace" button.

3. Type in the words, punctuation, or the like that you want to replace. If you want to delete the tabs, click "Ctrl" + "C," and "Ctrl" + "V" over a tabbed space in the document and in the "Replace With" window.

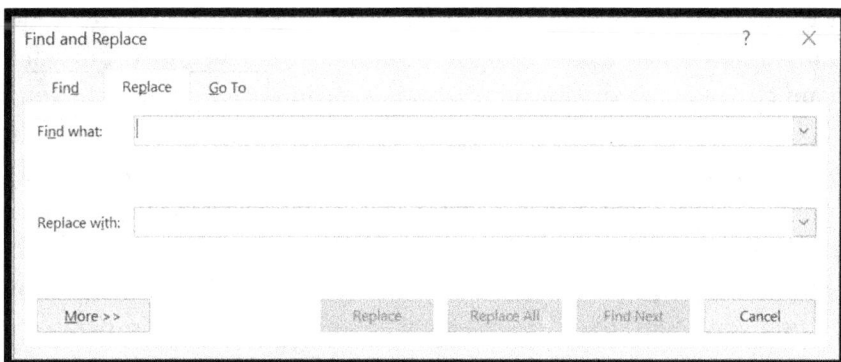

**Fig. 3.3. Word Replace Function**

Another common mistake that proofreaders should look out for is the relationship between quotation marks and punctuation near them. Commas, periods and other punctuation marks usually go on the interior of quotation marks. For example, the following is incorrect, "Here we go". The following is correct, "Here we go."

European writers and even some folks in America sometimes use 'single' quotation marks when a "double" quotation mark is appropriate. Remember that only quotes inside of quotes need only a single quotation mark. And in block quotes, double-quotation marks are used around text quoted in the block—the block itself does not need quotation marks around it.

*Note:* If you correct mistakes that aren't mistakes in the writers' writing—they might get upset and will COMPLAIN that they don't want to be working with interns, etc. (YAYKS!) If you don't notice some mistakes that are there, the writer might notice these later on after the formatting is completed, and this usually means a very difficult re-formatting job for the formatter or designer. So, try to find a balance, or simply look up any problems that you aren't sure about. It's a good idea for you to give yourself a grammar refresher course as you work on editing projects for Anaphora, or for any other publisher.

## How Much to Edit?

There are several degrees and varieties of editing methods, and the method you use is primarily determined by your ability and time limitations. If you are working as a volunteer, any help you can offer is much appreciated. But here are some definitions and explanations about what the various editing degrees are. A writer frequently requests one of these. The most commonly requested edit is a light proofreading, and this is what you should usually do, if the Editor doesn't send a request for one of the other options. Some writers would rather keep their work as-is, and others are happier with the maximum degree of editing. It's important to follow the writer's preferences. In general, it's a good idea to do heavier editing on the first and last pages of a book, and on the opening and closing paragraphs of each chapter because these are frequently read by those reviewing the book or thinking of buying it.

You can also help with formatting the document to prepare it for being turned into a book. Formatting in Word can be done at the same time as proofreading and editing, or afterwards. Additional formatting is later done in InDesign or Publisher, but most of the formatting can be preserved in the transfer, which significantly speeds up the production process. Some elements can't be done formatted in Word, such as captions, tables, and a few other elements.

Be sure to do a close edit of the writer's biography and summary or abstract, as well as the blurbs and all other key components that describe the book. The biography and summary are posted on the publisher's website, various other websites, and on the cover of the book. Thus, it is especially important that these are heavily proofread.

I credit all interns on the website for the work that they do as interns, and I can also offer proofreading or editing credits if you do a heavy proofreading or a heavy editing. Usually, very light proofreading is not credited. If you work for a major publishing house, definitely do not expect to receive a proofreading or editing credit, as even most in-house editors aren't credited.

I personally think creative and innovative re-writes are almost always a good idea, but I infrequently do them on book projects to avoid having my work go to waste. There is a lot heavier re-writing and ghost-writing going on in some of the bigger publishing houses, but folks there usually make $6,000+ per a heavy edit. Editors that work professionally, and only make light edits can make around $600 per project. So, only do heavy editing and re-writing work for Anaphora if it's fun for you—it is never a requirement. A volunteer shouldn't do $6,000 of work for free, unless they want to do it for practice or for fun. Also, the speed of editing/ proofreading should determine the level of editing you should do. If we are backed-up, light editing is more appropriate, if we are having a slow season, heavier editing might be OK. The same is likely to apply with other publishers, but you should always ask the manager for editing preferences.

*Light Proofreading*

Read over the manuscript, and change with track-changes the grammatical, spelling and other errors and typos that stand out. If there are any obvious mistakes with names, plot, story and other elements that stand out, insert a comment about the problem, or fix it, if this means changing only a few words here and there. Please do read the entire MS when doing any proofreading—the goal is to make sure buyers of the book won't have grounds to return it because of the typos/ lack of proofreading done on the project.

*Heavy Proofreading*

When doing heavy proofreading, in addition, to the steps you take in light proofreading, you read the MS more slowly, and pay attention to the style and the wording in the sentences and not only to obvious mistakes. Keep track-changes on, and feel free to delete repetitions, or even whole sentences that do not help the story or are badly written. Sometimes deleting even a whole paragraph might help the rest of the chapter to move forward more quickly. But, don't go too wild with the deletions, as most writers might feel attachment to some of the details even if the paragraph isn't moving quickly. Also, when deleting, make sure to delete any pertinent information to the story—such as, who's done it, etc. Basically, in heavy proofreading, you should keep the stylistic rules in *Elements of Style* in mind, and not only the rules of basic spelling and grammar. It is a good idea to have a book released from a well-known publisher on your desk, which is in the same genre as the project you are editing. This way, you can check the style in this published book against the style in the book you are editing.

*Light Editing*

When a writer requests light editing, they usually mean a light proofread as well as a bit of light editing. As you review the MS, for grammatical and spelling errors, also insert comments about ways the writer can improve the book, or in the story, before it goes to press. Keep in mind that if the book has already been accepted, the writer might not be willing to make many or any changes. So, it's a good idea to think about your comments and explain why the changes you are proposing are necessary. Also, only comment on things that definitely should or must be changed to make a commercial book. If you saw this book at a store, would you buy it? If not, why not? The answer to this question—should be present in your comments.

*Heavy Editing*

When doing heavy-editing, do everything you would do in a heavy proofreading and light editing, and in addition feel free to suggest much bigger changes. For example, should some chapters be deleted or grouped together? Are the parts of the book logically divided? Are some characters/ plot lines unnecessary? Are there things the writer can do to improve their style/ writing method throughout? Give them some pointers. Feel free to delete as many paragraphs/ sentences or even chapters as you'd like (keeping track-changes on). You might want to do some re-writing on the first and the last few pages of the project, to make sure that these are very polished and ready to be sold to readers.

*Academic Heavy Editing*

In addition to doing heavy editing and proofreading, if you are working on an academic or critical work, you should also check for a few elements that are only a concern in these types of projects.

1. Is the bibliography using 1 consistent bibliographic method? I prefer using MLA, but frequently chapter end notes in Chicago style are more practical and more readable in academic books. You should have a handbook for that style in your library, if you want on academic books, and double-check the citations.

2. Is the book readable and can it be understood by a general reader that's not familiar with the subject matter that's discussed in the project?

3. If the book is an edited dissertation—are all references to the dissertation deleted?

4. Is all evidence provided believable? Is the researcher making up or exaggerating their claims? If so, try to suggest corrections, and further research.

5. Do ideas connect and flow from one to the next? Does the writer introduce the content he or she is about to cover in a given chapter properly, so that you know where the chapter is going? Does the writer summarize what they proved in the chapter at the end? Are their logical chapter breaks that separate content of different sorts?

6. Is there an adequate introduction/ summary provided that

fully explains what the book is about, and that captures your interest in the project?

7. Are some parts confusing, difficult to read, contradictory, or otherwise nonsensical—try to fix these glitches, or leave a note asking for clarification—explaining what's confusing etc.

8. It's a good idea to do some research on Wikipedia or by other easily-accessible means when doing an edit of an academic work in a specialized field. This way, you will be somewhat familiar with the topic, and it should be easier for you to understand what the writer is trying to say.

*Editing Poetry, Novels, Short Stories and Other Odd Works*

While some books are written in a plain modern style, and can easily be edited with the help of *Elements of Style* or the like, there are some projects that will challenge the grammarians in you. For example, a poetry book, I recently published uses an e. e. cummings style of poetry and in this style there is a different set of grammatical and punctuation rules. Here's an example from *Mathematics of Love*:

**19**

**DISCOVERER**

First, the good line
finds its own
source—the sun,
moon or other
nourishment

: travels through
the bent finger
—continues its
adumbrations—
locates

In this case, the positioning of the lines or their spacing in relation to each other is more important than if the commas are in the right places. Still, if you read a post-modern poem, and find that it is nonsense, or there are clear logical fallacies/ problems, you should leave a note for the writer. The more post-modern the poetry is, the more careful you should be with changing it. You can still be very helpful if you notice typos/ spelling mistakes, but throw most rules of grammar out of the window.

You should also be aware of the genre your novel is written in. How do most fantasy vs. mystery novels start? You should give writers advice on how they can fit their chosen genre better. Avoid trying to make a fantasy more mystery-novel-like, etc.

## Re-Writing

As I mentioned earlier, there are several parts of an MS that might require re-writing: first and last few pages, biography, summary, beginnings of chapters and parts of the MS that have very severe problems of various sorts. Before re-writing, ask if you feel confident that you can do a better job than the writer has done. If you are sure that your re-write will improve the MS, and the writer has approved re-writes and other major changes—proceed, but be sure to change the color of this added heavily altered text, to let the writer double-check if they like your changes. There is always a chance that they might not like the changes and your work might have been wasted, unless the writer or the Editor-in-Chief specifically asked for a re-write.

## Formatting

There are some formatting mistakes that appear in most manuscripts, and some are uniquely weird to a given writer. Here are some ways you can improve the formatting of an MS at the same time as you do your proofreading/ editing:

1. Change the font throughout to one of the following most frequently-used fonts that you think is the best fit: Calisto MT, Bodoni MT, Cambria, Book Antique. In 2016, I started primarily using Adobe Garamond Pro, as it's a great fit for scholarly and literary books, and I'm using it in the new edition of this guide. The font should look good in a book and many

other Word fonts are not available in Bold/ Italic in InDesign, where I format the book. Courier New should be used only with scripts or script excerpts inside of the book. Change font size to 11pt throughout and to 16pt for the chapter titles, poem titles or other major headings. Feel free to change these titles to any font that would look good in a book, and change titles to all caps, unless the writer might have a reason for using another capitalization method on titles.

2.  If there is a "Table of Contents" in the MS, delete page numbers from this table. If there isn't a "Table of Contents" and there are poem titles or chapter titles (other than Chapter 1, 2, etc.), insert a "Table of Contents," but leave out page numbers next to the titles, as these will change when the book is formatted in InDesign.

3.  Change the spacing of the MS, so that it is single-spaced, without extra lines inserted between paragraphs.

4.  Paragraph indentation is one of the most annoying problems when formatting—here is a trick to fix it. A. Select a place that has been tabbed in the document and save it with "Ctrl+C" 2. Hit "Ctrl+ F" and replace the tab you've saved, hitting "Ctrl+V" with nothing in the "Replace" box. This will delete all tabs throughout the document. 3. Select the text of the entire document (you might want to do this 1 chapter at a time, as chapter titles and other headings shouldn't be indented), and move the top part of the ruler cone, so that the MS's paragraphs are all indented by .25" or ¼ of an inch. .25" is the standard paragraph indentation I use in 6X9" books. Don't delete tabs in poetry books or in other books where the tab has a useful function in the text.

5.  Block quotes and other oddly indented paragraphs: when you do the above change, you might want to be careful to skip doing it on paragraphs that are oddly indented. Block quotes are frequently indented not only on the first line, but throughout either by .25" or .5"—it should be consistently either .25" or .5" throughout. Sometimes, block quotes are also indented on the other side or on the right side of the lines—this is a stylistic

decision that's up to the formatter.

6. Works Cited and Bibliography pages are usually reverse-indented. If you aren't sure how a given part should be indented, check how it is done in a published book in a similar genre. Also check if the citations follow a common method such as MLA/ Chicago. Works Cited lists should be in a slightly smaller font than the rest of the document—10 or 9pt.

7. The first line in a new novel or critical book chapter should not be indented.

8. Delete page breaks between chapters, moving the next chapter to be around 6 lines after the preceding one, as these frequently don't transfer well in InDesign and it takes longer to delete lines when formatting in InDesign than it does when formatting in Word. There should be at least 2 lines between a chapter or another title and the first line of the section.

9. Chapter titles and all other formatting should be consistent throughout. If there are any chapters without titles among a group of chapters with titles, do insert suggested titles, and otherwise fix the formatting so that it's consistent.

## Blurb Acquisition

When a book is nearing the completion of the editing and proofreading stage, or once there is a PDF of what the interior of the book will look like, it's the best time to solicit back-cover blurbs from the writer's associates, who have some credits to their name that would make them into an authoritative judge of the book's content. Including blurbs on the back cover and in press releases is likely to increase the book's saleability and visibility. Blurbs can be a short phrase, or a full paragraph.

# STEP 4: TITLE SET-UP

O nce the reviewer or editor submits their suggested changes, the writer reviews the manuscript, and approves or objects to the changes and submits a cleaned up copy of the full manuscript and supporting parts. At this point the title is ready to be set up for the production process. There are three main steps that need to be taken at this point, before the formatting and design of the manuscript is begun.

1. Creating a Bowker ISBN listing is an option that only larger publishers that buy their own ISBN numbers should take. You might have problems using this website with Explorer, and should use an alternative web browser, such as Google Chrome. Go to: https://www.my-identifiers.com/. Click on the ISBN tab and select "Buy an ISBN." Buying in "Bulk" is for over 1,000 ISBNs at a time. You will see the following price options:

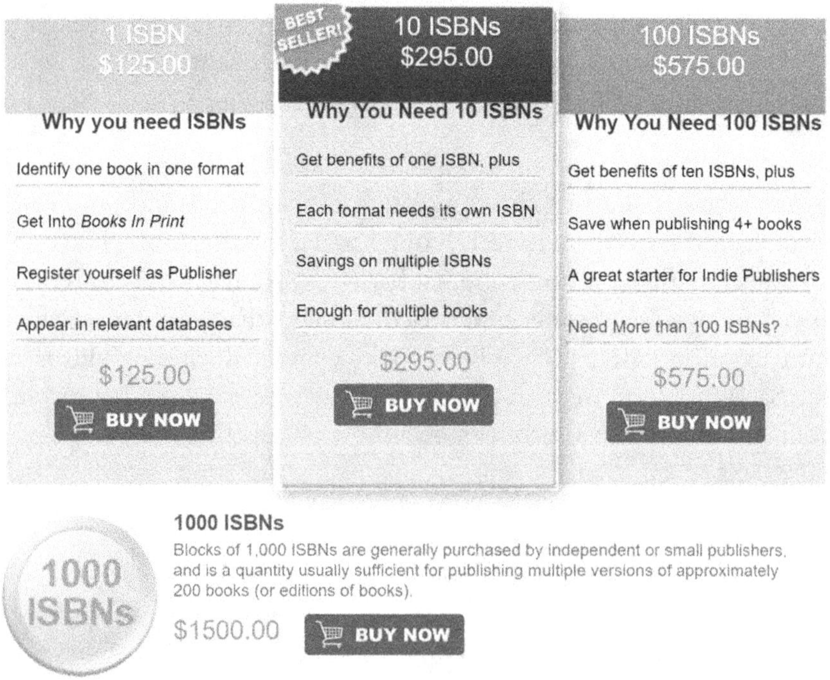

| 1 ISBN $125.00 | BEST SELLER! 10 ISBNs $295.00 | 100 ISBNs $575.00 |
|---|---|---|
| **Why you need ISBNs** | **Why You Need 10 ISBNs** | **Why You Need 100 ISBNs** |
| Identify one book in one format | Get benefits of one ISBN, plus | Get benefits of ten ISBNs, plus |
| Get Into *Books In Print* | Each format needs its own ISBN | Save when publishing 4+ books |
| Register yourself as Publisher | Savings on multiple ISBNs | A great starter for Indie Publishers |
| Appear in relevant databases | Enough for multiple books | Need More than 100 ISBNs? |
| $125.00 | $295.00 | $575.00 |
| 🛒 BUY NOW | 🛒 BUY NOW | 🛒 BUY NOW |

**1000 ISBNs**

1000 ISBNs

Blocks of 1,000 ISBNs are generally purchased by independent or small publishers, and is a quantity usually sufficient for publishing multiple versions of approximately 200 books (or editions of books).

$1500.00  🛒 BUY NOW

Fig. 4.1. ISBN Prices

Once you purchase the ISBN numbers, you will want to assign title information to a specific ISBN numbers, when you want to release a new title. You will have to create an account and will receive log-in information. When logged in, you will click on the "My Account" tab to access your ISBNs. Select "Manage ISBNs" from this tab. Click on "Assign Title" button. You will be taken to a series of 4 different pages that will ask you to enter information about your new title.

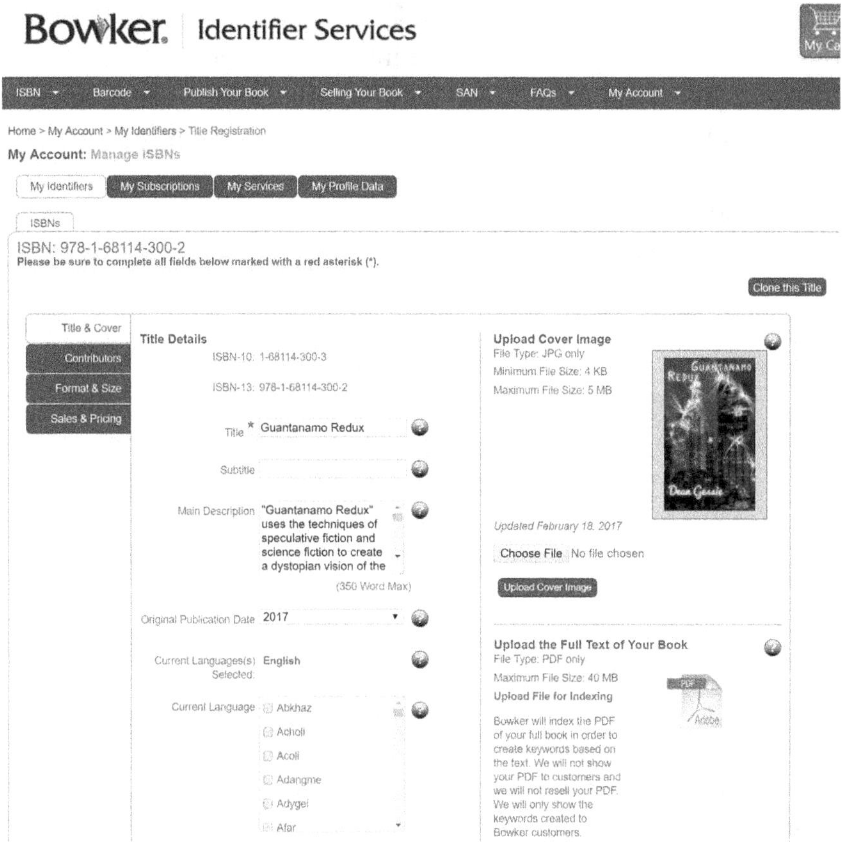

**Fig. 4.2. Bowker Title Set-Up**

The above image is what I see when I click on the ISBN information tab for this Publishing Guide. You'll notice that there is a space for the cover image, and below you can insert the entire content for your book, to make it more searchable in online search engines. The more information that you enter here, the higher your sales will be with distributors that might find your title in the Bowker catalogs.

Another thing for you to notice is that each ISBN number is really two numbers or rather the same number in two formats: the 10, and the 13-digit ISBN numbers. For this book title these numbers are:

ISBN-13: 978-1-937536-25-1
ISBN-10: 1-937536-25-4

The 6 digits in the middle of both of these is the number that will be consistent across all of the ISBNs you just purchased from Bowker—it is the publisher identification number. The other numbers represent the location of publication, the title information and other identifiers that help buyers to interpret the origin of the book.

When you get to the last page, the "Sales and Pricing" tab, you will be able to enter the countries where you want to sell your book and the corresponding prices. Currencies fluctuate frequently, so you should look up the current exchange rates for your title. There are several free currency converters online, like the XE Universal Currency Converter, located at http://www.xe.com/ucc/. You enter the amount in your currency that you want converted and choose the currency you want it converted to.

The "Pricing" tab also allows you to make the title "returnable." There is a chance that you might lose a significant amount of money if many customers return the title, so most publishers sign a returns addendum with writers, asking them to pay for all returned books, if they want to make the title "returnable."

Lastly, on the "Pricing" tab you specify if you have "exclusive" or "non-exclusive" rights to the title. Small publishers typically sign non-exclusive copyrights contracts with writers, and larger publishers usually ask for exclusive contracts. A non-exclusive contract means that the writer can sell their book to other publishers in print, electronic and other formats.

2. Once you have either assigned an ISBN# to a title or decided to use a free print-on-demand publisher assigned ISBN#, you are ready to set up your title in the printer's database. You should research which printer is the best fit for your needs. If you want to print 500+ copies, you probably want to research traditional printers, as they will offer discounts that beat the prices per-book offered by print-on-demand printers. Assuming that you plan on printing less than 500 copies, you want to compare sell-publishing printers with printers used by small presses. The top four current online print-on-demand services are:

Lulu, Blurb, Wordclay, and CreateSpace.

I initially considered printing with Lulu, but then set up over a dozen titles with www.CreateSpace.com. The printing quality with Createspace isn't great. I have had my books' covers peeling when exposed to sunshine or heat. In addition the binding process is problematic as the pages are difficult to keep opened in thicker books. Thus, interior margins have to be wide to accommodate the poor binding. But, I think they fixed these binding problems by switching to printing with Lightning Source. The benefits of using Createspace include the fact that they have great templates that allow for convenient book cover design. Another benefit is that CreateSpace is a subsidiary of Amazon, which means the titles go up on Amazon quickly and the "Look Inside" option is automatically added to all of your titles.

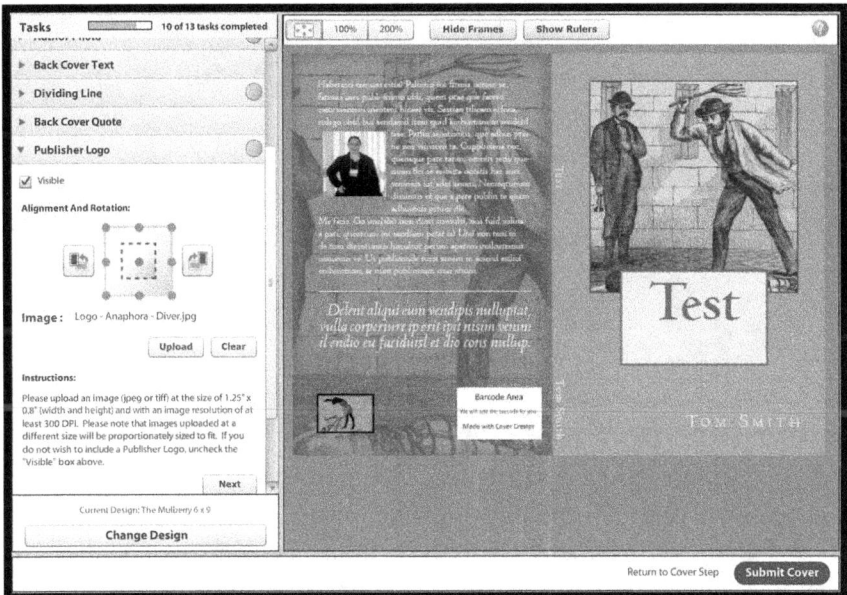

Fig. 4.3. CreateSpace Cover Set-Up

If you have a mid-sized press or a small press that prints at least 40 book copies per title, you will want to consider alternative publishers that do both POD and non-POD print runs. One of the most established printers in this category is a subsidiary of Ingram, Lightning Source (LS). It costs around $63 to set up a title with LS, but this cost is cut in half if your press is a member of the Independent Book Publishers Association, which offers a 50% discount for members. For a small 1-9 employee publisher the cost of IBPA membership is $129, which would pay for itself if you set up at least 4 different book titles with LS. There are some additional cataloging fees with LS, some of which are optional and others are required, and have to be paid annually. The catalog that LS uses is Ingram's, which means that you are cataloged in a source that's one of the most commonly used among librarians and other book buyers, so it's a good investment. In 2016, I was certified as a designer with Ingram and this cancels out setup fees.

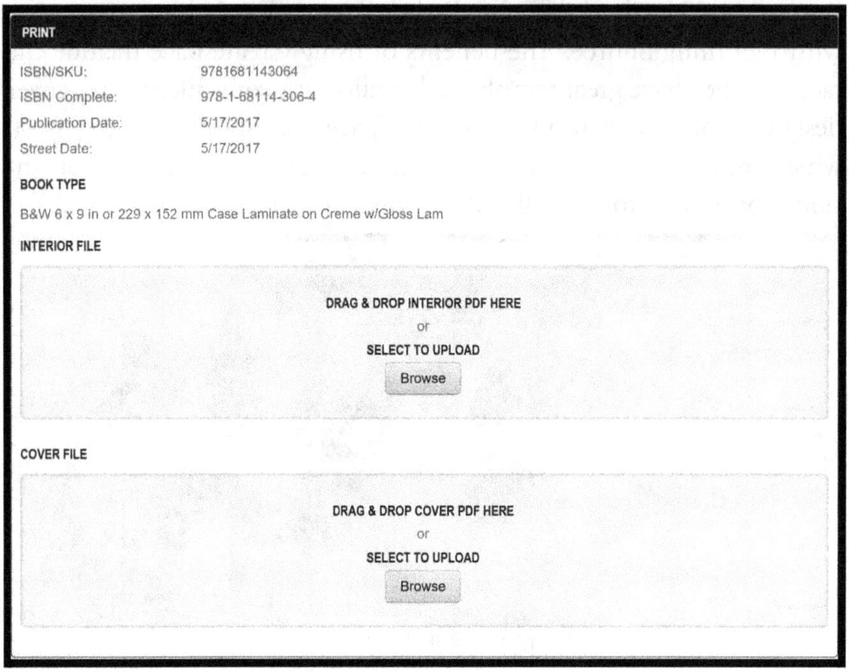

**PRINT**

| ISBN/SKU: | 9781681143064 |
| ISBN Complete: | 978-1-68114-306-4 |
| Publication Date: | 5/17/2017 |
| Street Date: | 5/17/2017 |

**BOOK TYPE**

B&W 6 x 9 in or 229 x 152 mm Case Laminate on Creme w/Gloss Lam

**INTERIOR FILE**

DRAG & DROP INTERIOR PDF HERE
or
SELECT TO UPLOAD
Browse

**COVER FILE**

DRAG & DROP COVER PDF HERE
or
SELECT TO UPLOAD
Browse

**Fig. 4.4. Lightning Source Title Set-Up**

By the time you create a listing in the printer's website, you should have the book description and author's biography to insert into the corresponding windows. The setup process is guided by the printer's website, and you will receive warning massages if you make any mistakes.

3. One of the things the printers will ask you for is an LCCN number for the title. Books can have a variety of different identifying numbers. I already discussed the ISBN numbers. A journal or another type of periodical usually has a single ISSN number, which is used to catalog it in libraries in the periodical section and under the same route shelf number. The shelf number or the standard 800.22 or the like number you usually see when you look for books in a library is added by the Li-

brary of Congress once the book goes through the LCCN number creation process and is cataloged by the US Library of Congress. Not all book titles that are assigned an LCCN# are assigned a library catalog number, but all are stored in the Library of Congress and become more accessible for purchase by acquisition librarians. To buy an LCCN# go to: https://ecips.loc.gov/pls/ecip/pubs_signon?system=pcn. Only book publishers can set up an account with this office. If you are a self-publisher, you won't be able to set up LCCN#s for your titles. Once you have an account, you will be able to enter information about each of your titles into this system. Click on "PCN Application" from the main screen to enter data for a new title. You must mail a copy of the book once it is printed to the Library of Congress for their catalog if you use this LCCN creation system.

# Publisher Information Change Request

**Click here for Instructions**

**U.S. Publisher**

| | |
|---|---|
| **Publishing House:** | **Anaphora Literary Press** |
| **Street or P.O. Box:** | 1898 Athens St. |
| **City:** | Brownsville **State:** TX ∨ **Zip Code:** 78520 - |
| **Phone:** | ( 470 ) 289-6395 **Fax:** ( ) |
| **Email:** | director@anaphoraliterary.com |
| **Homepage:** | https://anaphoraliterary.com |
| **ISBN Identifier:** | 68114 |

**Senior Officer**

**Fig. 4.5. Library of Congress LCCN Set-Up**

When your title is set up in these programs and you are familiar with the design and formatting standards that your printer prefers, you are ready to begin designing the book.

# STEP 5: BOOK COVER AND CONTENT DESIGN AND FORMATTING

For most print-on-demand printers, like CreateSpace, you can use any basic book-creation program, including Microsoft Word and Publisher. If you regularly use Word, this might be a convenient option for you. Here is what your layout might look like if you try creating a book with Word:

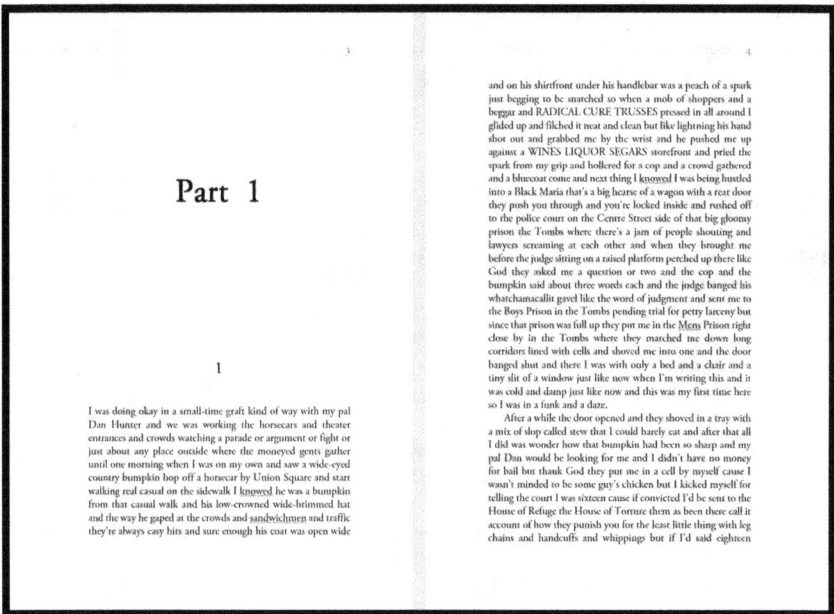

**Part 1**

1

I was doing okay in a small-time graft kind of way with my pal Dan Hunter and we was working the horsecars and theater entrances and crowds watching a parade or argument or fight or just about any place outside where the moneyed gents gather until one morning when I was on my own and saw a wide-eyed country bumpkin hop off a horsecar by Union Square and start walking real casual on the sidewalk I knowed he was a bumpkin from that casual walk and his low-crowned wide-brimmed hat and the way he gaped at the crowds and sandwichmen and traffic they're always easy hits and sure enough his coat was open wide

and on his shirtfront under his handlebar was a peach of a spark just begging to be snatched so when a mob of shoppers and a beggar and RADICAL CURE TRUSSES pressed in all around I glided up and filched it neat and clean but like lightning his hand shot out and grabbed me by the wrist and he pushed me up against a WINES LIQUOR SEGARS storefront and pried the spark from my grip and hollered for a cop and a crowd gathered and a bluecoat come and next thing I knowed I was being hustled into a Black Maria that's a big hearse of a wagon with a rear door they push you through and you're locked inside and rushed off to the police court on the Centre Street side of that big gloomy prison the Tombs where there's a jam of people shouting and lawyers screaming at each other and when they brought me before the judge sitting on a raised platform perched up there like God they asked me a question or two and the cop and the bumpkin said about three words each and the judge banged his whatchamacallit gavel like the word of judgment and sent me to the Boys Prison in the Tombs pending trial for petty larceny but since that prison was full up they put me in the Mens Prison right close by in the Tombs where they marched me down long corridors lined with cells and shoved me into one and the door banged shut and there I was with only a bed and a chair and a tiny slit of a window just like now when I'm writing this and it was cold and damp just like now and this was my first time here so I was in a funk and a daze.
After a while the door opened and they shoved in a tray with a mix of slop called stew that I could barely eat and after that all I did was wonder how that bumpkin had been so sharp and my pal Dan would be looking for me and I didn't have no money for bail but thank God they put me in a cell by myself cause I wasn't minded to be some guy's chicken but I kicked myself for telling the court I was sixteen cause if convicted I'd be sent to the House of Refuge the House of Torture them as been there call it account of how they punish you for the least little thing with leg chains and handcuffs and whippings but if I'd said eighteen

**Fig. 5.1. Book Interior Design in Word**

To create this, you simply go to the "Page Layout" tab. Under "Page Setup," click on "Size," and instead of the standard 8.5X11" page size, type in 6X9", 5.5X8.5" or another page size that you want to use for your book.

Then, you click on "Margins." Select "Custom Margins." Change the layout to "book fold," in order to have facing pages in book-form. I recommend using 1 inch margins on the interior. .25" margins on the exterior and on the bottom or the top of the page (wherever you will not insert a page # or another header/ footer). On the side with the header/ footer, you should have a .75" margin, so that you leave enough room for the header/ footer. The ideal margin sizes change for thicker books and depending on the printer's specifications. You should fit most book sizes and most printers if you allow for these wide interior margins.

For most books, you will at least want to format and design the interior in Publisher, which allows for more header/ footer and page design options than Word. Both are Microsoft programs, so if you use Word daily, learning how to use Publisher should be pretty easy. You might have to buy Publisher, if you didn't purchase a full set of Microsoft programs with your computer. Buy the education edition if you are affiliated with a school; it's a lot cheaper.

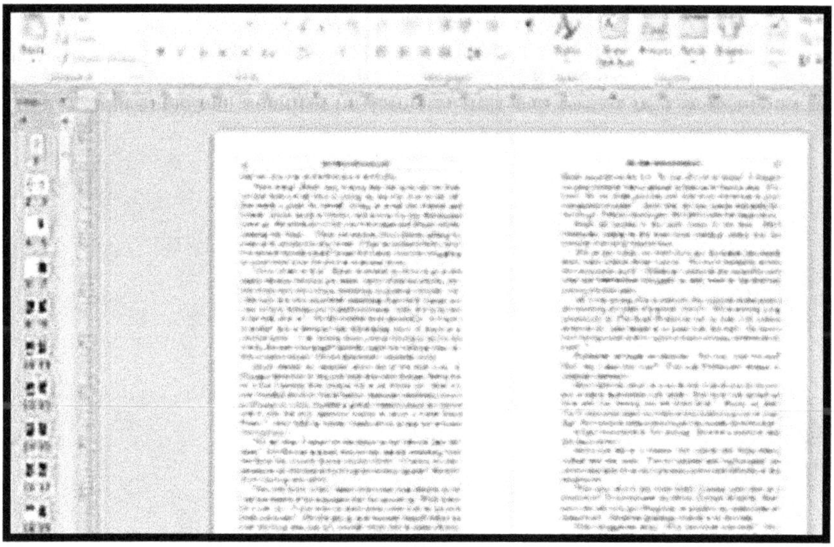

**Fig. 5.2. Book Interior Design in Publisher**

As you can see above, several buttons and options at the top of the screen are very similar to the options available in Word. The layout of the screen is different, and there are several additional formatting and design options that are not available in Word. You might want to buy a Dummies or another version of a book on how to use Publisher or InDesign, as there are several fine points to this process that can't be described here.

I will cover some InDesign basics because this is the program that some of my design interns might use to for interior book design. I would like to help them with the essential steps, in case they haven't attempted complete book design projects in the past.

## InDesign

InDesign is created by Adobe, which is known as one of the best design tools in the publishing industry. Most large publishing houses use Adobe products. Photoshop is one of these other products, and I'll discuss it when I discuss cover design. Typically, when designing and formatting a book, you will use three Adobe products: Photoshop, InDesign and Bridge. These are available in older and newer versions. You should be able to do the required basics with an older version, which is significantly cheaper. Once again, the "education editions" of Adobe products are also a lot cheaper than industrial products. If you are using these programs for the first time, you should use the Help menu to view training videos Adobe has on its website or on the websites of its affiliates.

Here are the steps to take to create a book in InDesign:

1. Click on "File."

2. Select "New."

3. Choose "Document." Don't choose "Book."

4. A window comes up where you will have the option to select or enter a new page size and the page margins. You might want to use inch measurements until you learn their pt equivalents. To use inches, for 6 inches type in, 6" and hit tab to move to the next value.

5. Anaphora interior design interns should receive a book template that is already formatted for the correct page and margin size, and includes set up Master pages that can easily be edited to fill in the specific information for a new book title. Poetry books need a slightly different book template, because the page numbers are usually at the bottom of the page in poetry books. Here is an example of what the template will look like:

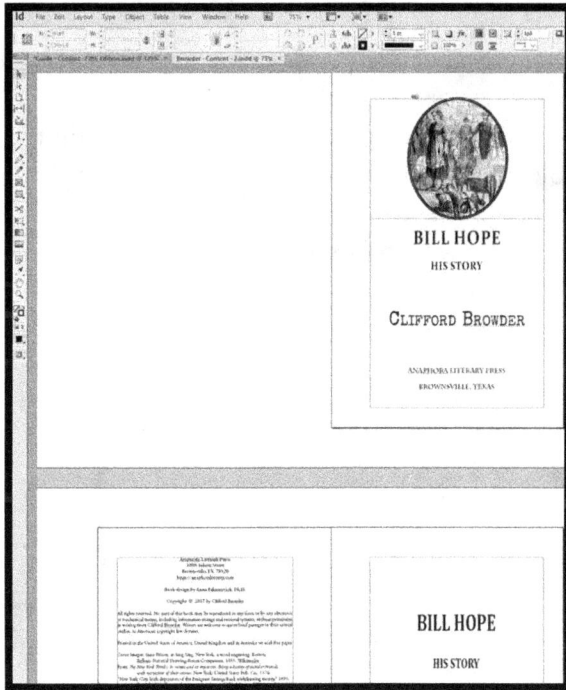

**Fig. 5.3. Front Pages Design with InDesign**

If your publisher sends a template like this one to you, here are the steps you should take to adjust the template to suite the book you are designing.

A. Before beginning save the template under a new name in the format, "Author's Last Name—Content." On the first single page, change the old title into the title of the book you are working on. Do the same for the author's name. Look through the first few title pages and change all of the author/ book title names into the names you see in the Word manuscript you received. The author/ book title names appear frequently, so look through the template closely.

B. Keep the same information for the publisher's name, location, etc. If you are designing/ formatting the book, insert your name in that section on the copyrights page.

C. If you have already found a cover photograph you plan to use, insert information about it into the copyrights page.

D. Insert the appropriate ISBN, LCCN#s into the copyrights page.

E. Remember that most of your sections will begin on the right-sided page. The table of contents should be on the right sided page, with one blank page between it and the title page:

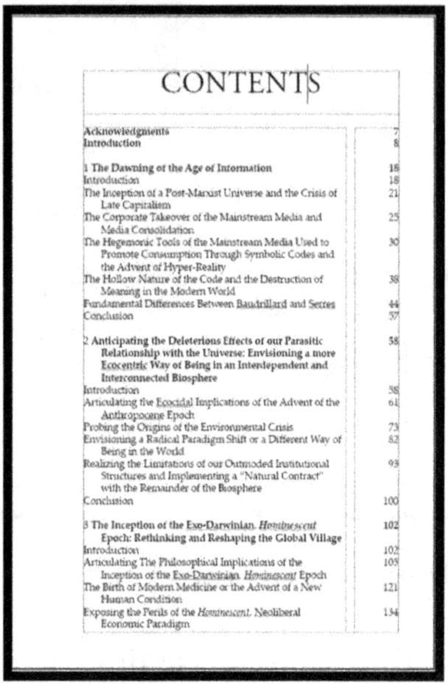

CONTENTS

Acknowledgments 7
Introduction 8

1 The Dawning of the Age of Information 18
Introduction 18
The Inception of a Post-Marxist Universe and the Crisis of Late Capitalism 21
The Corporate Takeover of the Mainstream Media and Media Consolidation 25
The Hegemonic Tools of the Mainstream Media Used to Promote Consumption Through Symbolic Codes and the Advent of Hyper-Reality 30
The Hollow Nature of the Code and the Destruction of Meaning in the Modern World 38
Fundamental Differences Between Baudrillard and Serres 44
Conclusion 57

2 Anticipating the Deleterious Effects of our Parasitic Relationship with the Universe: Envisioning a more Ecocentric Way of Being in an Interdependent and Interconnected Biosphere 58
Introduction 58
Articulating the Ecocidal Implications of the Advent of the Anthropocene Epoch 61
Probing the Origins of the Environmental Crisis 73
Envisioning a Radical Paradigm Shift or a Different Way of Being in the World 82
Realizing the Limitations of our Outmoded Institutional Structures and Implementing a "Natural Contract" with the Remainder of the Biosphere 93
Conclusion 100

3 The Inception of the Exo-Darwinian *Hominescent* Epoch: Rethinking and Reshaping the Global Village 102
Introduction 102
Articulating The Philosophical Implications of the Inception of the Exo-Darwinian *Hominescent* Epoch 105
The Birth of Modern Medicine or the Advent of a New Human Condition 121
Exposing the Perils of the *Hominescent*, Neoliberal Economic Paradigm 134

**Fig. 5.4. Table of Contents with InDesign**

If the book you are working on does not include a table of contents, this page should be populated with the first page of the manuscript, or any front matter, such as an acknowledgments page that the author might have included. When formatting the table of contents, create 3 text boxes. One is where the words "Table of Contents" or "Contents" is centered. The second is for the chapter/ section titles. The third is for the corresponding page numbers. This way you can left-indent the names of the chapters, and right-indent the page numbers.

F. Once the front matter is set up, it is time for you to paste in the formatted Word file of the manuscript. Before you can do this, there is one more step you should take. Open the Word manuscript, and make sure that it's in the right font, and that all of the front matter, like the author's biography and the title page have been deleted. Save the Word file with the title, "Author's Last Name—File Upload" and close it.

G. Now, click with the Selection Tool arrow on a text box in your file where you want to place the file upload text. Then, click on "File." Then click on "Place." Select the file you want to place, and double-click on it. A box of text will appear next to your curser. Direct the curser to the box you want the text to be placed in, and click anywhere in the box. The text will be inserted and will automatically overflow, adding pages to your document in a consecutive order. If instead of taking these steps, you Copy and Paste the text from a Word file, Italic, Bold and other types of formatting will not be preserved, and you will have to re-insert it across the file. You should check that the formatting has been properly preserved before continuing.

H. The next step, is formatting the chapters' or poems' titles by clicking on TT to make them into all-capital letters. You should leave 2 lines before a chapter title, and 2 lines after it before the chapter text begins. The first lines in a chapter should not be indented. All of the following lines should be indented by .25". Look through the document to check that there aren't any formatting errors and to otherwise clean up the file. Fix any glitches/ problems you notice. Avoid doing heavy proofreading or editing at this point, as writers frequently want to be notified with track-changes comments when major changes are made to their books.

I. You might want to insert a black-and-white image cut-out of the cover image into the first page of the document at this point, jumping forward to choose and Photoshop the cover image into 1 color version, and 1 black-and-white version of the same image. The black-and-white version goes into this interior, and the color version is for the book cover. You might want to turn the lower image upside down, or otherwise use special affects to make that first page visually appealing.

J. When you finish positioning and formatting the text, you should insert a header for most books, or a footer with only the page number for poetry books. You will have to adjust the standard template to have a wider bottom margin and a .25" upper margin when you format poetry books. For all other books, the template will include two Master pages: A-Master and B-Master. The A-Master is the page margins and shouldn't be manipulated. B-Master is used to insert page numbers and title information at the top of the pages in the book.

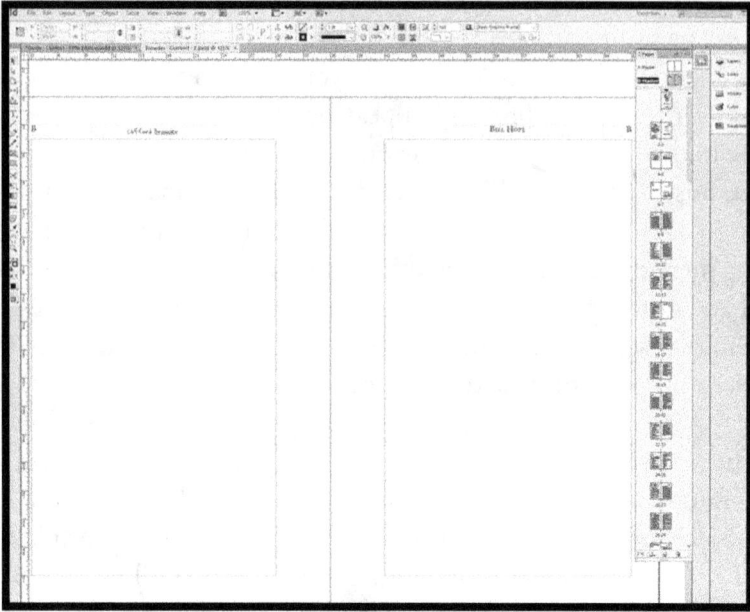

**Fig. 5.5. Master Pages with InDesign**

B-master for this book is displayed above. The "Bs" in the corners stand for the page numbers, which have automatically been inserted into this B-master template. You can keep these as they are, or change the font they are in. The centered boxes usually include the name of the book and the author's name. If you are formatting a journal, these might include information about the volume and issue number, and each chapter might have a different author's name in this box. If you want to change the information in these boxes in different sections of the book, you have to create additional masters, like C-Master and D-Master, and enter this varying information. Then, you would have to apply different masters to different pages. For a basic book, you only have a single master you use to insert header/ footer information. To apply B-master to pages, write out somewhere the page numbers you want to apply the B-master to. You don't want to apply B-master to the title pages, or to the first page, where Chapter 1 starts. You don't want to have any B-master headers on any blank pages, or on any pages that include information about the publisher of the book. And you might want to avoid including B-Masters on the first page of each of the chapters, though this is optional, depending on your design preferences, and on the book-type. Once you look over your document and select the pages you want to apply B-master to, you select, holding "Ctrl" the two pages of the B-master and right click on them with your mouse. Then, select, "Apply Master to Pages." A box will come up that will ask you to which pages you want to apply the B-master, and here you type the pages you decided on.

K. Now click on the "Pages" tab and select, holding the "Ctrl" key all of the remaining blank pages in the document. Right click on one of them and select, "Delete Page." The final document should have an even number of pages. To keep the page count even, you should keep one or two blank pages before the "Other Titles by Anaphora" or a corresponding concluding page.

L. When all this is done, you want to return to the "Table of Contents" and insert the appropriate page numbers for each section of the book.

## E-Books Design and Formatting

One of the new developments for Anaphora since the third edition of this guide has been the introduction of an electronic book option. In my experience academic and literary electronic books are very difficult to sell, while mainstream or flashy and easy to read books sell pretty easily, especially when they are set at $2.99 or less. But, it is an enormous and growing market, so it demands participation, and I've started making attempts in this direction. Along the way, I've discovered several formatting and publishing issues that are particular to E-Books and I'll summarize these here.

There are two programs that are typically used for making E-Book versions. The easiest option for somebody using InDesign for designing the interior is transforming the book into an E-Book in InDesign. The two most commonly used E-Book formats are .epub and .mobi. You don't need any extra programs to make the .epub version. Simply select "File", then "Export", then select the "Save as Type" option called, "EPUB". You will be able to make a few adjustments, including inserting Metadata, such as your publishing company's name, as well as your preferred image resolution (low, medium or high: this affects the size of the file and image quality). Most importantly, under "Advanced" options, you can choose to "Include Embedded fonts" or not. If you included embedded fonts, and your E-Book distributor gives you an error message, the first thing to try is to exclude embedded fonts, but this will create some glitches with your fonts, or can delete fancy fonts from your file. When you are done selecting options, click "OK" to run the conversion to .epub.

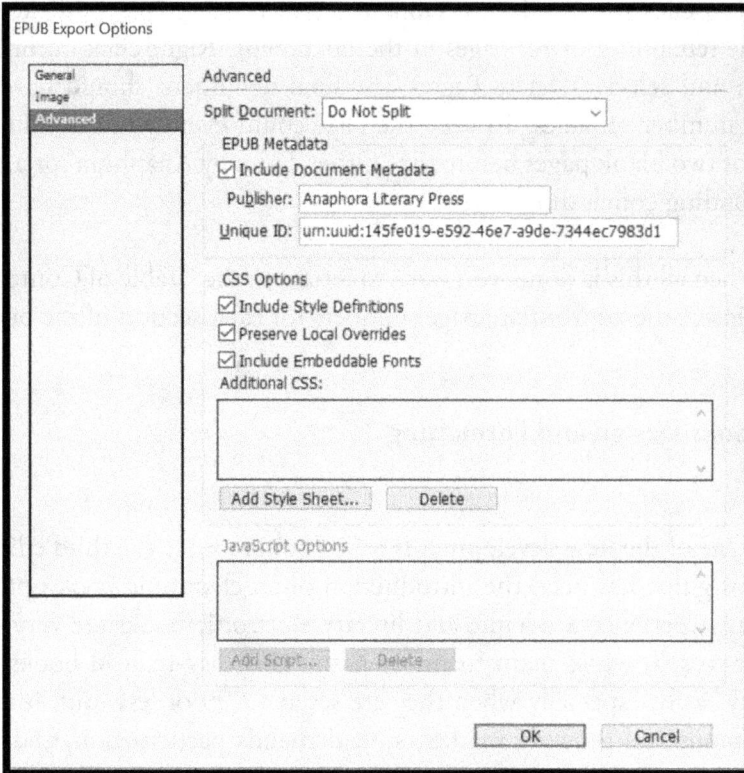

**Fig. 5.6. Embedded Fonts Option: InDesign**

To create .mobi files with InDesign, you will need the Kindle Plugin for Adobe InDesign, which you can download for free from Amazon. Once it's installed, you will see the option to "Export for Kindle" on the "File" menu. You will have an option to upload a cover image, adjust image resolution and to embed or not to embed fonts when you setup this export.

Remember to take out the page numbers from your Table of Contents in InDesign before running these conversions, as the page numbers in the E-Book will change, and your printed version page numbers will no longer be accurate.

The basic .mobi file is required by Kindle if you release a Kindle Edition directly with them. The .epub file is required by Nook Press, if you release an E-Book version directly with that division of Barnes and Noble.

I was doing these simple exports for a few titles when I started to contemplate how other Kindle and Nook titles have a clickable Table of Contents that takes browsers to different sections of the book. I considered releasing my E-Books with Ingram's Spark E-Book conversion division, but they charge a good deal of money for setup and don't assist with creating links. Additional research, led me to the distribution program that many independent presses have been utilizing across the last several years, Smashwords. They do not charge setup fees for basic distribution and transfer Word documents into every common E-Book file type, including .epub and .mobi. They have an option for publishers to also upload their own version of an .epub file that they create with InDesign, but in my experience, there are too many glitches possible with this option and it should be avoided. The best approach is to take the formatted text out of InDesign via Copy and Paste it into a new Word document. Re-insert all images separately, after you insert the text.

There are a few important changes you'll need to make in your file to prepare it for Smashwords' premium distribution to a dozen different E-Book reader devices. First, instead of your usual Copyrights Page content, you'll need to insert the special wording that Smashwords requires, which will be similar to this:

**The Romances of George Sand**

Anna Faktorovich

Published by Anaphora Literary Press at Smashwords

Copyright 2014 Anna Faktorovich

Smashwords Edition

This ebook is licensed for your personal enjoyment only. This ebook may not be re-sold or given away to other people. If you would like to share this book with another person, please purchase an additional copy for each recipient. If you're reading this book and did not purchase it, or it was not purchased for your use only, then please return to your favorite ebook retailer and purchase your own copy. Thank you for respecting the hard work of this author.

The back matter of your book, can include the following components:

**Discover other titles by Anna Faktorovich...**

**Connect with Me:**
Follow me on Twitter: https://twitter.com/AnnaFaktorovich
Friend me on Facebook: https://www.facebook.com/anna.faktorovich
Subscribe to my blog: http://anaphoraliterary.com
Favorite me at Smashwords: http://www.smashwords.com/profile/view/faktorovich

Thank you for reading my book. If you enjoyed it, I hope you will take a moment to leave me a review at your favorite retailer?

Thanks!
Anna Faktorovich

The biggest change you'll need to make to prepare the book will be adding a clickable Table of Contents. To do this, select the title of each of your chapters, and click on "Insert", then "Bookmark", type a simple name for the section, such as "Ch1", and then click on "Add". After you've created Bookmarks for all of your chapters, and all other clickable sections, create a Contents list after the Front Matter, as in:

Contents

Chapter 1
Chapter 2

Then, select the first item in this table, "Chapter 1" and click on "Insert", then "Hyperlink", and then select the "Place in This Document" option, and select "Ch1" to link that spot in the file with the Table of Contents. Do the same with each of the other sections in this Table.

Once you have the formatted Word file, you'll set up the title information in Smashwords and will upload a Front Cover and this formatted and bookmarked file into their system.

# STEP 6: COVER IMAGE EDITING

Before you can begin designing the cover, you have to find and edit the cover image. Some writers prefer that artists they know or have hired choose the image or design the entire cover. Assuming that the writer has left this choice up to the publisher, the designer's job is to sift through the various images and to choose one that is right for that specific book project.

There are a few things to keep in mind when choosing images. First, you want to make sure that the image is in the public domain or does not have any restrictions on its copyrights, and specifically is available for commercial editing of the image and the sale of the finished product. Many archives that hold visual images, charge hundreds of dollars for the reproduction of a piece in their collection in a book, and even more when it is on the cover of a book. You should avoid these options. There are plenty of free images out there, and your job is to find the best fit.

The second thing to think about is what search terms, or categories of art you should look for. Look back at the book summary and at some of the works in the book. Do they suggest a theme, or an artistic style for the cover? You might want to go online or to your bookshelf and look at similar books and the type of cover art that's used on them.

Anaphora has compiled a list of 100 possible cover copyrights-free images on a Google Documents account that can be shared with writers. Writers can then choose the images that fit their book. If they don't find something on this shared site, Anaphora looks for specific art works that might work, or asks the writer to help with the search.

Remember to download the highest resolution of the image that's available, preferably a TIFF image, unless the TIFF is too large to easily e-mail. The next-best type of images are JPEGs. The image should be large enough, so that it doesn't become blurry and pixilated when the resolution is increased during image editing.

## Available Sources of Copyrights-Free Art

1. *Pixabay*: This is perhaps the largest database of free photographs, art, vectors, and various other materials that are indispensable in book design. Photographers upload photos that they might not think are salable on paid websites here. While paid images might be of a higher quality, or might be better executed, somebody who is skilled with Photoshop and other image editing software should be able to edit out the imperfections and escalate these works to a status fit for a great cover.

2. *Google Images*: These are frequently a last resort because it's too difficult to screen out images that are not in the public domain or might come with a resolution that is too low for a professional design.

3. *Creative Commons*: includes several image search engines, including Google Images and Flickr.

4. *GettyImages*: The best of these are not free, but there is a public domain section that includes some great options.

5. *Library of Congress* (Prints and Photographs Online Catalog): This is a good source for scholarly books that require exact maps, or photographs of historical individuals. The images here are better for book interiors rather than for the cover because most of them are black and white. The quality and resolution of the images that are available are usually outstanding, as there are tiff and very detailed jpeg versions.

6. *Wikimedia Images*: If you are searching for classical art in the public domain and you don't mind having a somewhat low resolution, it is relatively easy to find a specific artist or genre of art in the Wikimedia database.

8. *New York Public Library: Public Domain Collection*: In 2017, they are advertising 180,000 images in the public domain, making them one of the largest public library collections of free images.

9. *National Gallery of Art*: Any fan of very complex, classical art should enjoy looking through this rich collection of some of the world's top art. There is a good deal of public domain, free options here. It might be difficult to find something fit for a pop novel, but there are plenty of historical periods covered to fit various subjects.

10. *Yale University Art Gallery*: This is another source for outstanding art.

Once you find the right image, record the information about the image and place it into the content interior book document. You typically want to include: the name of the artist, the title of the picture, the location the art was made/ the picture was taken, the place the work was created and the collection where it might currently be held.

The second thing you should do is save the largest version of the image that's available into your files. If the image is too small or has a very low resolution to begin with, it is likely to come out pixilated, when the book is printed.

**Photoshop Editing**

Before you can insert your chosen picture into the cover template, you must edit the image in Photoshop to make sure it confirms with the necessary dimensions. Photoshop can open various types of files: jpeg, pdf, etc. You should choose the format that your cover design program can work with. For example, you can't insert pdf documents into Publisher. jpeg images work well with most types of design programs.

The most important thing to fix in your picture in Photoshop is the file size and resolution. The resolution must be at least 300 dpi or ppi and the length should be 9". To change these, click on the "Image" tab. Then, click on "Image Size." You will see the window below. The "Resolution" line should read 300. I usually change it to 400 to be on the safe side. If your picture is for the front cover only, and you plan to use a different image on the back cover, the length should be 9" and the width around 6" for a 6X9" book. If your image is horizontal and you want to stretch it across the back and front cover parts, the width should be at least 12" and the height is the same at 9". Make sure that

"Constant Proportions" is checked, so that the pixels will automatically adjust and the width: height dimensions remain constant. Most pictures won't be exactly 6X9", so you want to change the height to 9" and then crop or otherwise manipulate the image to fit with the template.

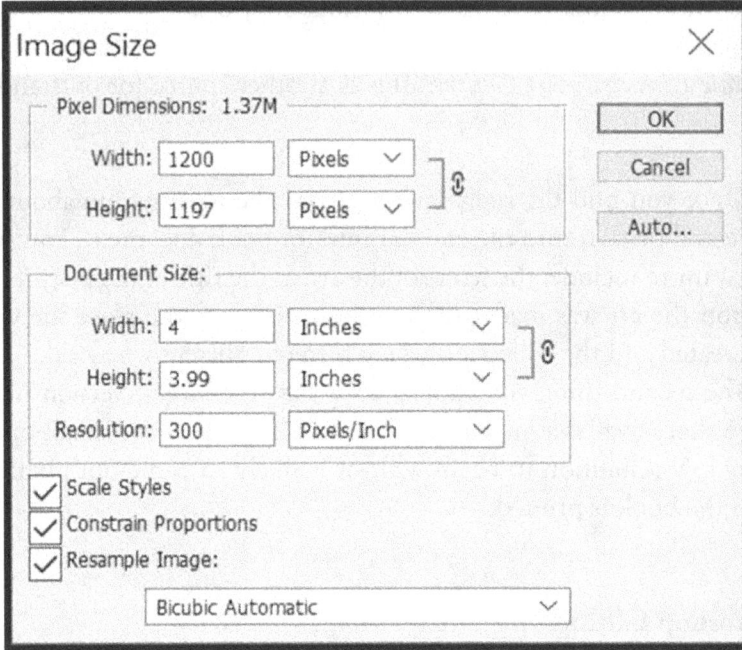

**Fig. 6.1. Photoshop Resolution and Size Editing**

There are various types of image editing that you can do with Photoshop, and even more options with the more recent CS5 and CS6 Photoshop options. If you are not familiar with Photoshop, it is essential that you find a basic guide on Photoshop before attempting any advanced image editing with this program. This is what a CS6 Photoshop window looks like.

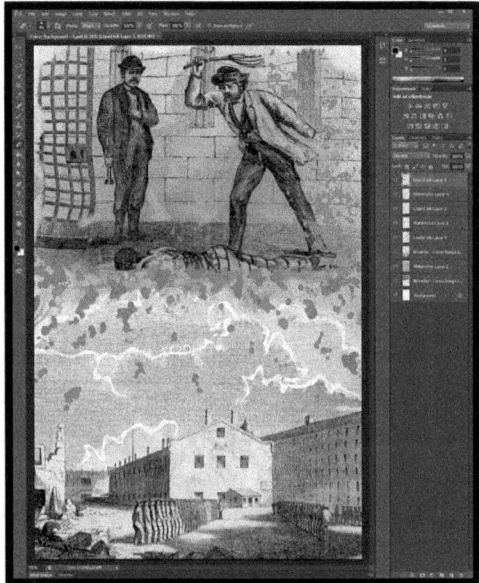

**Fig. 6.2. Photoshop CS6 Main Window**

And here are a few examples of images edited with Photoshop:

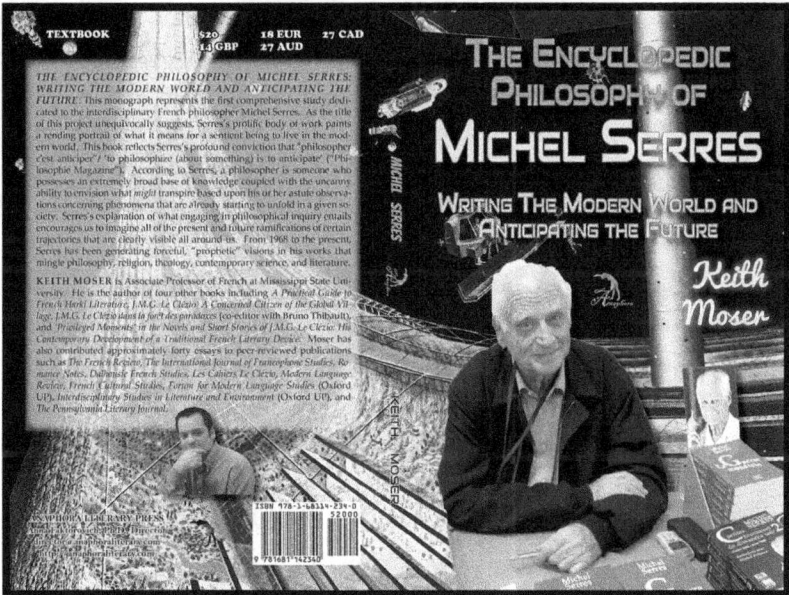

Fig. 6.3. Cover Design for Keith Moser's Book

Fig. 6.4. Gessie's Cover Edit in Corel Painter 2017

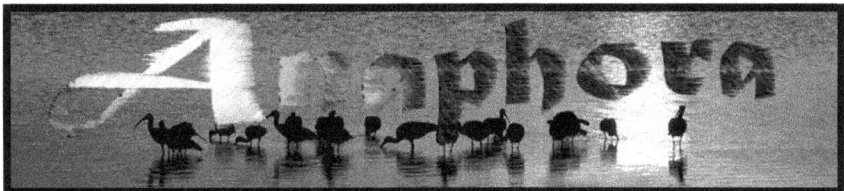

Fig. 6.5. Anaphora Website Header Design

As you can see, you can add text over images. Add vibrancy and color intensity to images. Change image color. Insert camera glare. Change a photograph into a water-color styled picture, and otherwise add texture and variety that was not in the original image you found. More recent versions of Photoshop, allow for intense image corrections, which allow you to insert "Content Fill" in place of objects you want deleted from a given image. Unnecessary objects and imperfections can be smoothed away during the image editing stage.

In 2016, I started experimenting with Corel Painter 2017, and inserted the image I drew for Gessie's cover into Figure 6.4 in place of a previous Photoshop design. Painter allows for more original and paint-like modifications of photographs as well as completely new drawings. Photoshop's paintbrushes always look digital, but Painter has water-color and other realistic brush types that can fool the observer into thinking they are done with real paint. It also includes elements like fire, ice and other dynamic bits that are fit for special effects. There are also some basic photograph to painting tools that can add mystique and romance to a pretty basic photograph. So, with enough time and patience, Corel's Painter can add a lot of creativity to a book's design.

This is the creative part of the job, where the designer can have fun with the medium. But, a good design should remember to look at sample image types from books in the genre they are working in, to stay in the bounds of fitting artistic experimentation.

# STEP 7: COVER AND CONTENT INDESIGN FORMATTING

Upon completing the interior content formatting, you should turn that document into a PDFx1a document. You shouldn't take this step before all parts of the interior are finished. To make this conversion:

1. Click on "File"

2. Click on "Adobe PDF Presets"

3. Click on "PDF/X-1a: 2001"

4. Click on "Save"

5. Click on "Export"

You might receive some error correction messages. You should click "OK," or on the appropriate option. A PDF is generated:

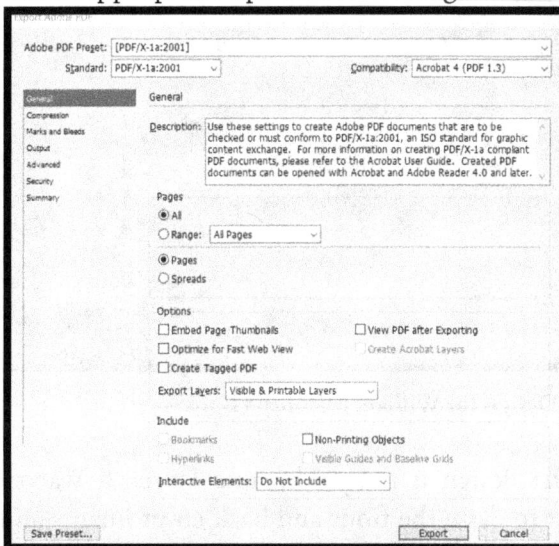

**Fig. 7.1. PDF/X-1a: 2001 Creation with InDesign**

## Advanced Photoshop Editing

Once you feel confident with the basic photo editing techniques, you can try to mimic some of the advanced image and text editing and creation techniques that can be executed with Photoshop. Let's look at four of the covers I designed recently and the techniques I used in these designs.

The cover design below is from a 2017 release, an adventure novel by William Maloney. This is an example of a cover that combines a couple of public domain photographs from Pixabay, with some added flare in the fonts. I previously included a collage from Susan Case's cover here, where I combined photos of Elvis, the Beatles and other musicians. Each of the photographs was on a separate layer in Photoshop. Both Case's and Maloney's covers were built similarly, with images positioned and edited separately and then the entire image is combined in InDesign or another program.

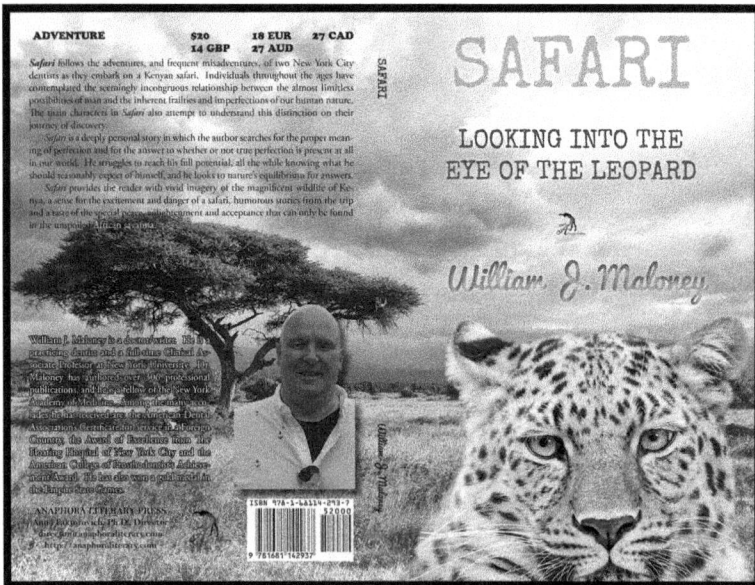

**Fig. 6.6. Cover Design for William Maloney's Book**

This next cover design is unique because I used a Wacom Bamboo drawing tablet to draw the front and back cover images and all of the images that appear inside of this book. With the popularity of iPads and Kindles, there have been several recent advances in electronic drawing technology in recent years. Last time I attempted electronic drawing was back in 1995, when I got my first Windows PC computer. I used the mouse to doodle in a basic Paint application. The lines were square and I only had one basic line texture that I could use. In contrast, today one can buy a drawing tablet with a screen as large as 8X6" for as low as $45, though professional artists shouldn't buy a tablet that costs less than $200, as those in the higher price range are more likely to be pressure-sensitive and to have a surface that is more responsible to a wireless pen. I bought two, and the cheap one from China caused a system crash that forced me to do a full recovery on my computer. Photoshop allows artists several additional drawing tools, such as a variety of different brush types, and paint textures. I used a grass-style brush with a regular thin brush over it in the front cover *The Sloths and I* text.

Keep in mind that the final file-size for detailed drawings done entirely in Photoshop is very large, at around 120,000 KB. So, you will probably need a USB with 64GB+ of storage capacity.

Overall, this is a great time to be a digital cartoonist.

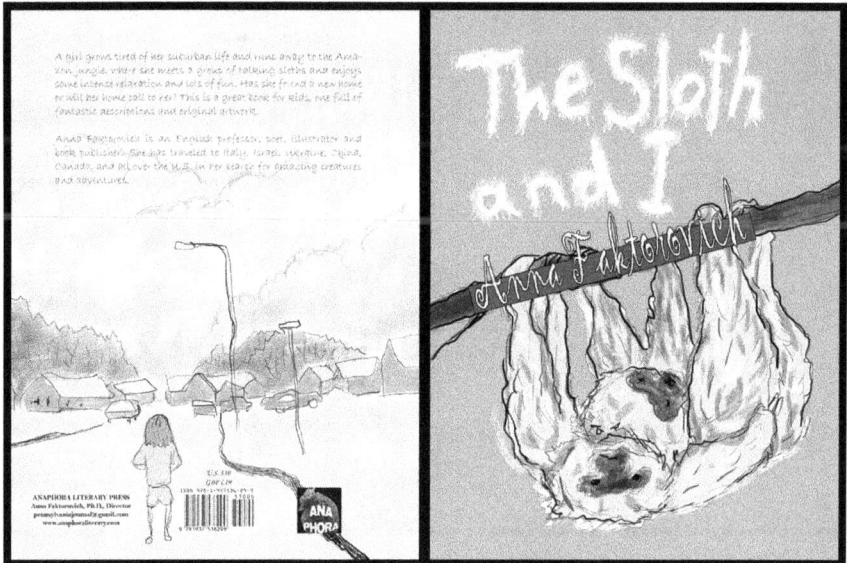

**Fig. 6.7. Cover Design for Anna Faktorovich's *Sloth* Book**

Of course, few popular book covers include original art that spans the entire cover image, and many include small drawn elements that enhance the photographs, shapes or classical art in the background. For Robert Hauptman's autobiography, I took a color photograph of Bob standing on a snowy mountain. Then, I took a black and white photograph of Bob and his wife when they were young. I created two versions of the BW image, one of Bob and the other of his wife, deleting the backgrounds and all other content from these images. I then inserted each of these BW images as separate layers into the color mountain image. I made these layers somewhat transparent to give them a ghostly, from-the-past feel. Finally, I drew over all of these images extra clouds and outlines to bring these images together into a single composition. At the end, I moved the final image into InDesign and inserted the text over it.

This is a great example of how you can merge digital text and image manipulation with hand-drawing in a cover design. If you only use a photograph or a classical work of art, the cover might look too simplistic, and if your drawings skills aren't at the expert level, merging the two techniques is a beneficial alternative.

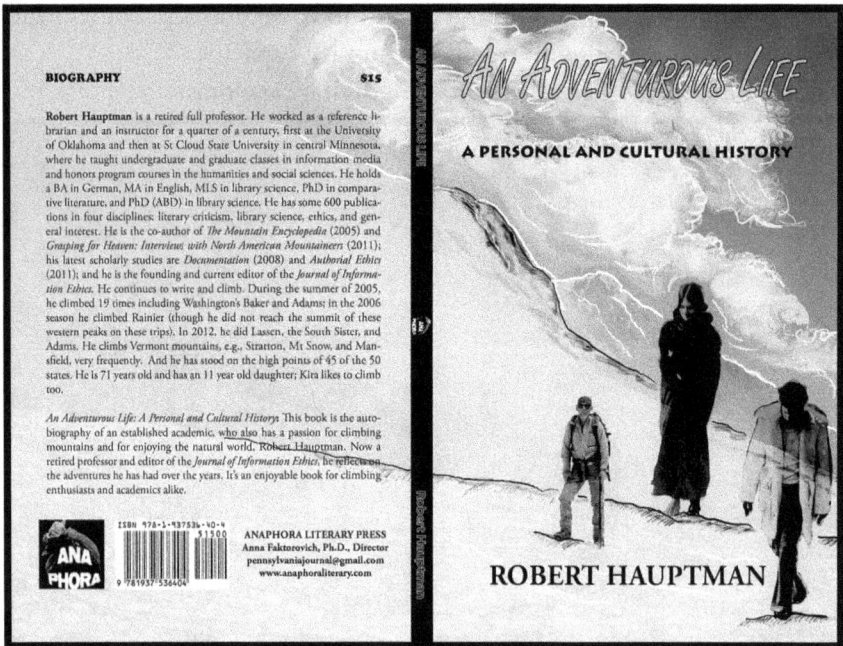

**Fig. 6.8. Cover Design for Robert Hauptman's Book**

Another approach for blending painting and photographs is by tracing over photographs in Photoshop. This can be achieved by creating a new layer and then deleting the original photograph, or by adding elements to the image in the photograph. For Lucas Carpenter's cover

I went to the Saguaro National Park, around the Mica Mountain. It's a park surrounded by a mountain range and that is covered with exotic desert plants and wildlife. I took a couple hundred digital photographs with my smart-phone, and also did some tablet drawings in Photoshop to get a feel for the texture of the landscape. I realized that my photographs were stronger than the drawings, but that the drawings were more original. So, when I got home I did an experiment where I opened one of the photos in Photoshop, added a new layer over it and did a thin-brush drawing over the outlines of the main shapes. Then, I deleted the background photo, and drew with different brushes in color over the outlines until I had the image you see below. Modern artists frequently utilize tracing techniques to position realistic drawings, and you can try this approach in one of your covers for a unique affect. You might also want to warp or manipulate the photo before tracing the counters for a cartoonish look.

For Mark Spitzer's cover, I decreased the density of the image, so that the yellow base color overshadowed the green plants in the background. I matched the color in the lettering to the other elements, so that there was flow and balance in the image. This is a special case where the author purchased the photograph on the cover, so it was outstanding and did not need much Photoshopping.

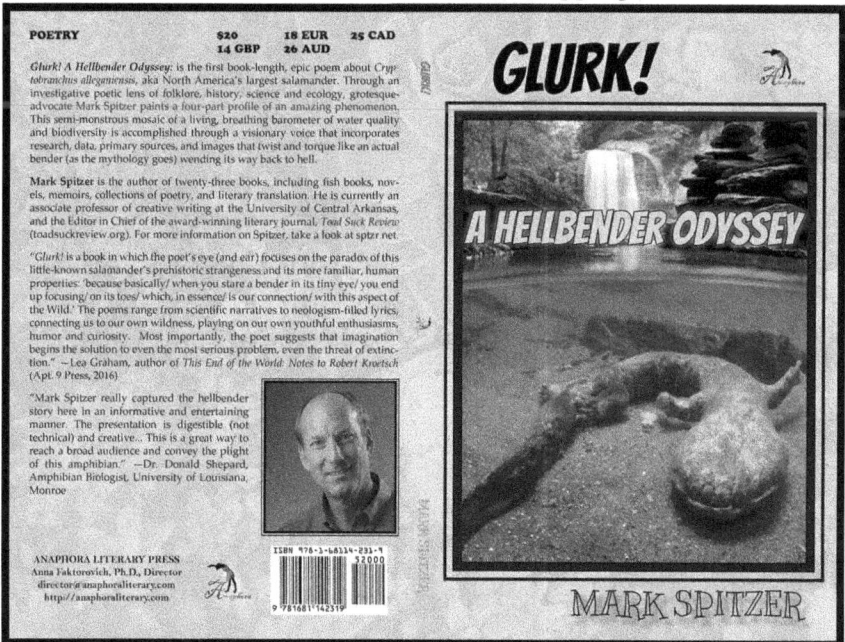

**Fig. 6.9. Cover Design for Lucas Carpenter's Book**

The PDF/X-1a standard is required by Lightning Source. Some print-on-demand printers can create a book out of a simple PDF file, and do not need this specific format type. Most printers will accept PDF/X-1a files and this file type helps you avoid several formatting/ design problems, like the need to embed fonts, etc.

## Cover Design

The appropriate style and type of cover design depends on the printer you are using. CreateSpace has an online cover design option, which allows for a quick and convenient cover generation process. Lightning Source requires that the cover text, images and the rest be placed over the template that they generate based on the # of pages in a given book title. When you have created the PDF/X-1a file, e-mail it to the publisher, or upload it to the Lightning Source website and then access the Lightning Source's cover template generator (or ask the publisher to generate one).

To generate a cover on the Lightning Source website, from the main screen, under "Tools," click on "Cover Template Generator." The following screen will come up. You fill in the requested information, and click on "Submit." The template is emailed to the provided address in an InDesign or a PDF format.

Then, you insert the images and text over the parts of the template that are going to be visible **Fig. 7.2. Lightning Source Cover Template Creation** in the finished printed book. As in the following example that follows.

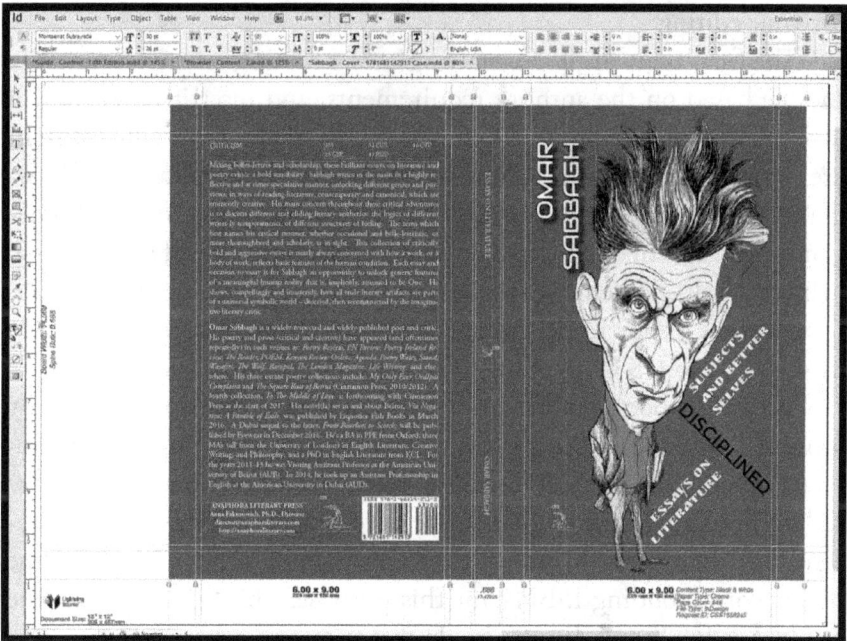

**Fig. 7.3. Sabbagh Cover in InDesign**

As you can see, the size of the page is larger than the cover. Don't delete the remainder of the template. Lightning Source (unlike CreateSpace) wants to have this full 12X15" template, so that they can cut the cover out of it using their programs. This is a template for a hardcover.

The standard parts to place on the cover are: book title, author's name, publisher's logo, publisher's information, author's biography and book summary or review quotes about the book. Most books also have the author's name and book title sideways on the spine. The template should specify if the book is too thin, and cannot have any text on the spine. The ISBN barcode has to be left visible on the back cover. You might want to add a "Feather" or a "Transparency" "Effect" to the back cover text, or a white/ black background to make this smaller text easier to read. If any parts of the cover look pixilated, you should edit the images in Photoshop to increase their resolution.

Convert the finished cover into a PDF/X-1a file, just like you converted the interior content. E-mail these two PDF files to the publisher. The publisher is likely to e-mail these files to the writer for his or her approval and final proofreading. So you should also e-mail the InDesign versions of these files, so the publisher would be able to make final changes, if they are too small to forward the project back to you for your editing.

The final steps in the formatting/ design process include updating the file based on the author's requirements, and inserting LCCN#, if it is missing at this point. Then, the PDFs of the cover and content are submitted to Lightning Source for review. No physical proof is ordered. Lightning Source provides free electronic proof copies. (Sometimes there are small glitches between the electronic proof and the final printed book). When Lightning Source approves the book, the publisher orders a copy for its collection. Then, the publisher mails a copy of the book to US Copyrights Office, which provided the LCCN.

When the book's information becomes listed on Amazon (usually around 2 weeks after the book is published with the printer), the publisher uploads the cover and content to Amazon Look Inside, at http:// sellercentral.amazon.com. The front cover image and the interior content files are merged in Acrobat into a single PDF file with the name of the corresponding ISBN# for this purpose. This upload makes the book have the Search Inside the Book option in its Amazon page.

The next step is inserting the information about the book's 1. Author and 2. Title into the https://anaphoraliterary.com website. A separate page is created for the author where this information is also included.

To be thorough, the book's publication information can be updated in Bowker's ISBN website. https://www.myidentifiers.com/.

The book is now "published" and if the author ordered discount copies, they are mailed to him or her. Now it's time to market and sell the book.

# STEP 8: PREPARING FOR A MARKETING CAMPAIGN

Selling books is a job which when left to chance is not likely to be productive. If the author does not participate in the marketing and sales process, it is likely that a literary book might not sell any copies beyond the discount copies the author purchases upon the book's publication. Most authors, once they publish 40+ books at a discounted price, are interested in selling at least those 40 copies to come out with a profit from the project. There are several steps the author and the publisher can take to make sure that a significant number of books sell.

1. *Book Review Copies Mailings:* If the author asks for this service, they purchase at least 5 copies of their book at the standard 25% off the cover price discount and have them mailed to the publisher for processing. Typically the author provides the addresses of the reviewers that they would like to send the book to. The publisher can also help this process by providing a list of some of the reviewers in the book's field who have previously reviewed the publisher's titles. Anaphora's previous book reviews are including in the "Press Clippings" tab of the Anaphora website. These book review copies are typically sent with a press release and a letter that are specially designed for that title. The letter is created in Word with an Anaphora header and footer and the press release is created in Publisher. You can use a Publisher template or create a unique design for the release. Both the press release and the letter have to include accurate information about the reviewers mailing address, and the book's information (ISBN#, ISSN#, distribution channels, etc). You should always look at examples of recent press releases for the required information to include here before creating a press release for a new title. Here are examples of a typical letter and press release.

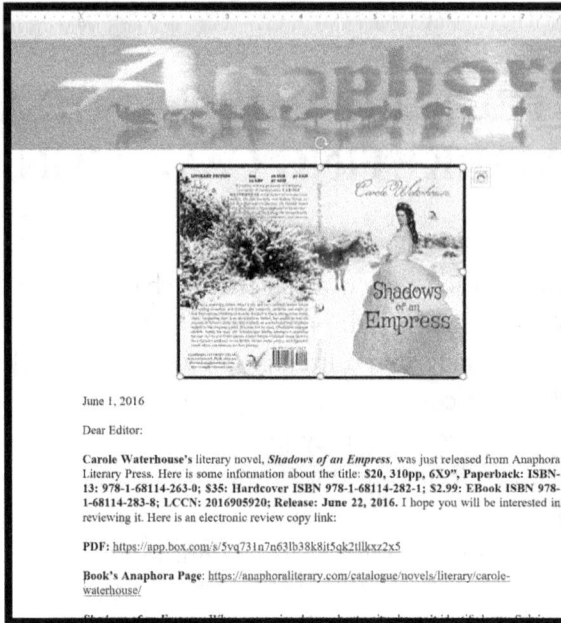

**Fig. 8.1. Book Review Request Letter**

In addition, to sending books for review, the press release and letter can be useful for sending notices of publication to the local media outlets. Local newspapers, radio programs and other venues are likely to write pieces about the writer or to invite them to participate in other promotional opportunities upon receiving an emailed or a mailed press release. The press release also frequently helps writers to set up book readings in their local bookstores. These readings

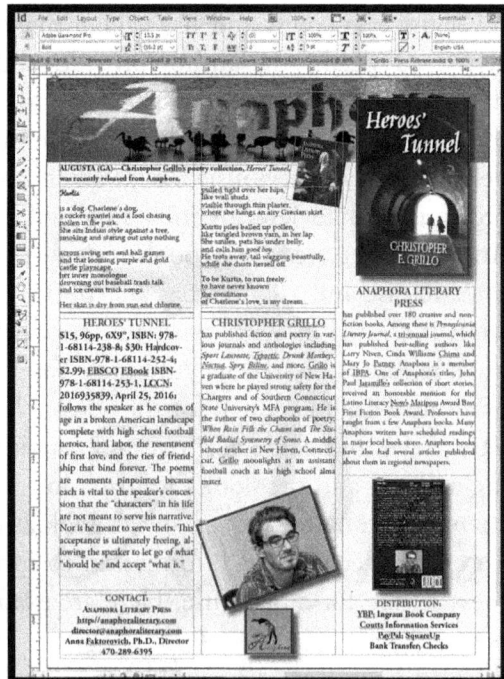

**Fig. 8.2. Press Release Design with InDesign**

can lead to a few dozen or more book sales, if properly advertised. The information about past and upcoming author signings and readings is posted on the Anaphora website.

Besides press releases, writers should also improve their online presence. Solicit book reviews to be posted by your friends and coworkers, or professional writers on the Amazon page for your book. All writers should set up an author's page on Amazon. Publishers can't set up an author's page for you. Writers should also use their standard social media (Facebook, LinkedIn, GoodReads, LibraryThing, and the like) sites to advertise their upcoming or release book.

**Advance Review Copies**

While some reviewers accept print or electronic copies of a book after it has been published, the best and biggest reviewers only review books that are mailed to them 1-4 months prior to the publication date. *Publisher's Weekly* and the *Library Journal* are two of these reviewers. *New York Times* and most other major newspapers and magazines state on their website that they only review books sent to them in advance. Think practically about your book. Is there a chance these bigger reviewers will publish a review about your book? If you think that they might, and if there are no deadlines you might miss by waiting, it is probably a good idea to delay the publication of your book by 1-4 months after it is ready to go into print. Here are the steps of this process:

1. *Pre-Release Title Set-Up*: The publisher sets up the book with an ISBN, LCCN numbers and the like. The book is designed and formatted as usual. The book is sent to the printer. The printer, such as Lighting Source, sets it up for short-run printing. The printer does not post it on Amazon, or on other distribution sites. The publisher creates a page on its website for the book, listing it as forthcoming for a future publication date. And some websites, like Bowker, will list it with the future publication date that you intend to release it on.

2. *Pre-Orders and Review Copy Mailing*: The writer or the publisher orders copies to be sent out for review with a press release and a letter. You might want to pre-order some books for your own use, such as to

show to bookstores to schedule future readings. Review the information about the types of review copies that a given source requires before sending them out. They might need 3 copies, or they might need an electronic copy. Follow their directions.

3. *Waiting Period*: Then, the writer and publisher wait for 4 months between the time they send review copies and the publication date. Once the publication date arrives, they contact the printer and ask to "release" the book and make it available for distribution and public sale. The writer and publisher might want to solicit Amazon and other alternative reviews during this period.

4. *Distributor Discounts and Returns*: Right before you schedule to release the book might be the final chance to adjust the distributer discount rate and other parts of the book. In general, sales are likely to be higher if the book is returnable, and has a 50% discount for distributors. Your publisher might have a "returns" addendum or a returns section in your contract that states that the writer is responsible for all of the costs associated with returned books. The percentage of returned books might be small if you print the books POD, but might be a lot larger if you run a huge print-run and attempt to distribute it to national discount stores.

5. *Publicizing a Book Launch*: The author in collaboration with the publisher, or independently might want to schedule a book launch. Before the launch date, send a press release to the local media (and perhaps to news wire and other advertising sources) about the event. Putting together a book launch or a big reading for everybody you know will help sell any copies you might have purchased at a discount from the publisher (or might have received for free if that's the publisher's policy).

## Promotional Materials

Some writers set up readings and signings at regional or national events, and request signs, business cards and other promotional materials with the Anaphora name on them to display at their booth or table. There are several printers that print these materials. I typically use the Staples Print Shop. It can print various types of merchandise, including a six-foot display sign. Go to: http://print.staples.com/ to set up your order. I typically design and set up the materials with a given titles information and then give the writer log-in information and they pay for and ship materials to themselves.

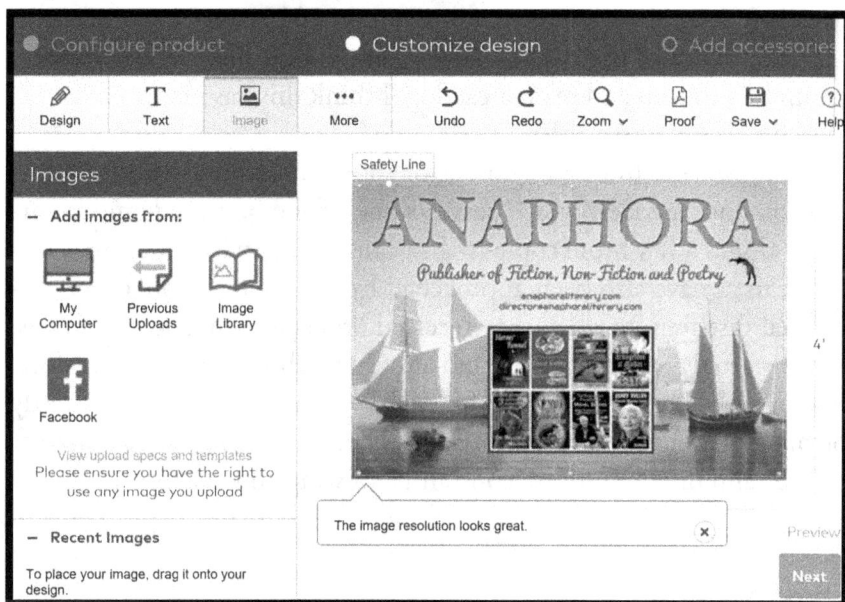

**Fig. 8.3. Banner Set-Up with VistaPrints Customized Designs**

In 2015, I started using VistaPrints and other online shops to print marketing materials because their quality is better and their prices are cheaper than Staples. The difference might be the result of their investment in just a few giant printers and then shipping products internationally, while Staples primarily works out of the printers they can fit into physical stores. The above is how a giant 6X4 foot banner looked as I was designing it in VistaPrints for my ALA exhibit. Well, the design has to happen in InDesign, and then the exact required dimensions, resolution, image type (RGB or CMYK) is uploaded into these platforms. Most of these marketing print shops offer plenty of templates for those who need help with the design, but a personalized brand message should really be delivered by providing all of your own unique elements. The background and stylistic embellishments can possibly come out of the public domain.

Once a publisher has at least ten titles, it is a good idea to start creating a catalog to send to libraries. Writers might want to buy a copy or two of this catalog (or might want a free copy). At first, I made this catalog as a PDF that could be downloaded from the website, and printed a few copies to give out at trade shows to potential buyers or interested authors. This catalog is now 48 pages, and I'm constantly placing older titles in the list of small icons in the back because with over 200 titles, these pages are filling up. In 2015 or so, I started mailing 200 copies of the catalog out to the top US libraries at a cost of around $4 to ship and print a catalog. I think this has increased overall sales for all Anaphora titles.

A few of the titles are chosen for special distribution with Coutts Information Services, which serves some of the best academic libraries, and sells a few more copies than I can manage without them. Over the years, I have also been approached by Follett and some other specialized distributors when they received orders for Anaphora's releases. I also started selling EBSCO and ProQuest ebooks, but these efforts have not been particularly fruitful. It's always a good idea to constantly be on a look out for new opportunities because publishing is a market in flux, and distributors are constantly growing and collapsing.

## Direct Sales Campaign

For a publishing house to increase overall sales, it is important to establish sales relationships with libraries, bookstores and other regular book buyers. If a publisher has a list of a couple hundred libraries that regularly buy their new releases, they can transition from a POD to a more standard printing and distribution model, as they have some guaranteed sales. But, this is a difficult transition to make because most major academic libraries already have established relationships with the top university presses and the top popular presses. So, they only purchase a few independent titles and typically need to be individually approached with a new publisher sales proposal. This section will give step-by-step instructions for launching a campaign that would solicit direct purchases.

1. *Creating a Marketing List:* Create an Excel file with the following column titles:

| Library Name | Acquisition Librarian's Name | Email Address | Phone Number |
|---|---|---|---|
| Pima County Libr. | Dr. Sam Goodman, Director | sam.goodman@pi.com | 520-440-6600 |

| Date: 1st Email | Date: 1st Call | Reply/ Status | Order Details |
|---|---|---|---|
| 3/11/2013 | 3/18/2013 | Ordered 10 | Different titles |

**Fig. 8.4. Excel Sales Contact List Titles**

It is important that as you create this list, you enter information in each of these key columns. You can add additional columns if as you begin the campaign you find that you enter the same type of information into the "Order Details" column. The library's and the acquisition librarian's names are especially important because a different marketing or sales representative is likely to make future follow-up calls, and they will need to contact the same person as you, so that they will reach somebody who is familiar with the exchange. The email should be used in the initial contact, and the phone number will come in handy in the follow-up call. The dates when the first and second contacts were made are significant because the timing of these calls makes a difference. The follow-up call shouldn't be made too soon or too late after the initial email. These dates will also help the supervisor to keep track of completed tasks, as a lack of a date in one of these columns signifies that a given contact hasn't yet been initiated. The "Reply/ Status" column will help future representatives to avoid contacting any contacts that definitely do not want to purchase any current or future titles from the publisher. It will also help to guide them with any specific requests an interested party might have made. All key mailing or order-type directions should be included in the "Order Details" column, so that orders are shipped without any glitches.

It should be noted that while these columns are titled with librarians in mind, they can also be used for creating marketing lists for bookstore owners, or other types of potential buyers. Mega bookstores have applications that need to be filled out, which requires a different approach. Small bookstores infrequently buy independent titles through cold-calling. Therefore, this section is primarily intended for finding and contacting libraries.

There are several sources with information on potential large-scale book buyers. The first 100 names on this list should come from the American Library Association's "The Nation's Largest Libraries: A Listing By Volumes Held", available online at http://www.ala.org/tools/libfactsheets/alalibraryfactsheet22. This is a great list because the biggest libraries are likely to have a big enough budget to afford buying several titles from an independent publisher. Of course, you should look through this list carefully. For example, the first item on the list is the Library of Congress, and it usually recieves titles from publishers for free, so it shouldn't be contacted in a marketing campaign. Nearly all of the other titles are great matches for any publisher. This list only includes the libraries' names, so you should copy and paste the names into Google to obtain the specific contact information you will need for your Excel data sheet.

Even if all 100 of the top libraries buy a publisher's titles, 100 sales per book is a pretty small number, so your sales list should preferably be expanded to include a couple thousand contacts. One way to reach this goal is with the help of Libcat: A Guide to Library Resources on the Internet, available at http://www.librarysites.info/. You should click on one state on the map at a time and by following the links collect the contact information for all of the libraries in a given state before moving on to the next state. Ideally you will organize the states in an alphabetical order, so that future users of your list will be able to navigate it with ease. Take your time with obtaining the exact contact information, as it will be time-consuming for future users to double-check your work, a task they will have to do if they encounter broken email addresses or other glitches with your list.

Once this general list is in place, future users will be able to add specialized buyers for individual new titles, or to expand this list in new directions.

*2. Preparing Marketing Materials:* With the list in place, you can proceed to the next stage in the marketing campaign. Before you begin contacting anybody, prepare the documents you will be sending out. You will need: A. A JPEG press release with the basic information about your press and some of the key titles you are trying to sell. The beginning of this chapter discussed the techniques you can use for creating appealing press releases. B. A PDF catalog of all of the forthcoming and released titles by your press. C. A letter of inquiry that explains why you are contacting the buyer and that gives some additional information about the press and the titles the press is offering. You might also need additional files, such as a sample PDF of a book your press has published, or an extra press release for one of your top titles. But, it's a good idea to keep the size of the initial email small, so that it wouldn't bounce from mailboxes that cannot accept large files.

*3. Contacting Potential Buyers:* You will need Outlook for the email campaign because it allows users to insert images into the text of emails, as well as other text and image manipulations. Sending individual emails to each of the contacts might be a better approach, even if it is time-consuming, as it makes it less likely that your email will end up in the Spam folder, which is designed to detect mass-emailing to several different contacts. In addition, individual emails will allow you to address each of your letters directly to a specific Acquisition Librarian and to insert a specific library's name at the top of your email. Having these details in the email will come in handy if you receive replies from librarians, as they will make it easier for you to identify in your marketing list the person that is replying to your email. Also, including the Librarian's name is likely to route the email to the right person, and the Librarian is likely to have a better feeling about your professional demeanor if you are addressing them by-name. In each of your emails, insert a catchy Subject line, such as "Independent Anaphora Literary Press Selling Great Titles." The line should specify the reason for your email and should include some specific information about your venture. The JPEG of the press release should be inserted after the text of your letter, and the PDF of the catalog should be attached to the email. After hitting send, record the email date in your Excel record-keeping file.

It's a good idea to wait for a week after your initial contact date before doing a follow-up call to the librarians. When you do the follow-up calls, open your Excel file and use the phone number provided. Ask for the Acquisition Librarian on your list, and summarize the email you sent a week earlier. Explain that you are calling to follow-up on that email and to inquire if the library is interested in buying any titles from your publisher. If they are, take detailed notes on their request, and forward these to your supervisor to handle to completion of the sale (unless the Librarian knows exactly what they want and you can answer all of their questions). If the librarian is uncertain about a purchase, or is leaning towards a "no," ask them if they would like you to mail a printed catalog to them or a sample of one of your press's stronger titles for free for a review. If the library agrees, take down their mailing instructions and forward these to the supervisor.

The Librarian is likely to have several questions that might need to be addressed by a supervisor, if the following list of likely questions and answers (specific for Anaphora) doesn't fit:

*A. Is the listed price in the catalog the retail press, and if so, what discount can we receive?* Yes it is, libraries receive a 40% discount, and the discount can be a bit higher if you have a different required standard discount. The discount price does not include shipping, which varies depending on the number of copies ordered and the location where the books will be sent.

*B. Which distributors does your press use? My library can't purchase books directly from a publisher.* Anaphora uses several distributors, including: Lighting Source, Baker & Taylor, Ingram Book Company, and Coutts Information Services. You can also buy individual copies through on-line bookstores, like Amazon and Barnes and Nobles. For the fastest delivery, you should order titles directly from Anaphora, especially if you are order 5 or more copies of one or multiple titles. Anaphora can accept PayPal, electronic bank transfers and check payments. There is a 4% extra charge with a PayPal payment. All checks can be mailed directly to Anaphora's mailing address, provided on the press releases and on the press's website. (You should give the details of the mailing address, if the Librarian asks for the details.)

*C. Our library only buys forthcoming titles, not those already in print.* Would you like to receive emails that would notify you of future forthcoming titles? And, did you see some of the titles in the catalog that are forthcoming in future months?

If you encounter an unusual question, forward it to the supervisor, so that it and its answer can be added to this list.

At the end of the conversation with the Librarian, ask them if they have any (other) questions for you? Then, thank them for their time and express your appreciation for their continued consideration, or for their purchase.

Enter the pertinent details into the Excel file, and once you finish your work for the day email the updated list as an attachment to the supervisor for their review of your progress. In this email ask any questions that came up during your interactions.

# STEP 9: MARKETING LISTS

## FREE PRESS RELEASE SITES

Have you ever wondered why so many newspapers (local, regional and national) carry very similar stories? Well, imagine if you got a job as a reporter at your regional newspaper. And I must admit that I have done just that for a few different papers. I, personally, preferred to go to political, cultural and social meetings, record the scene, question those at the scene and other old-school reporting techniques. But for reporters who write formulaically with a deadline in mind or who have gone to that same street fair every year for two decades, a speedier approach might be appealing. He or she could just call or e-mail the participants, but they might not be available, or might not want to be interviewed. But if he or she goes on a press release site, they find thousands of recent events in their area and around the world simplified into specific summaries of what has or will happen. Some detailed press releases are really press packets and include pictures, interviews with participants, long summaries, and just about all of the other information a reporter might need to write a newspaper article from the comfort of their home. It might be a *New York Times* reporter that cuts close to a deadline, or it might be somebody from a local paper. Thus, a writer that submits releases to these press release sites increases their chances that a newspaper somewhere will publish a piece about them. You might want to invest into submitting a colorful or a slightly more expensive release, as it's likely that the flashier releases will be noticed first. It's especially a good idea to submit a release, if you are giving a reading, or if there is something unique, unusual or otherwise newsworthy about your book. But you really just have to explain how your book is unique; it doesn't have to be something that has never been done before. The standard elements of a good press release are: book summary, author's biography paragraph, book cover image, the book's ISBN/LCCN#s, and distribution methods.

The following list was longer in the fourth edition of this guide, but I am cutting it down for this version. The interns that helped me generate the initial list did a great job finding the various paid and unpaid options available across the web. Since that time, I have only been submitting press releases to free PR websites. I believe there are enough of these around to make a news story visible. The costlier options might generate more interest from the press, but I have never attempted to employ them, so I can't recommend or berate them. I have a philosophy that good journalists will go out of their way to search for stories on free sites because they'll know that people with small budgets are likely to have more integrity, but perhaps this is just my hope rather than a reality.

The best benefits I have seen from posting releases on these sites are some articles on speedy news websites that reprint entire releases, and some visibility for the news in Google searches (if you search for the book's title or author's name).

**Free Press Release**
http://www.free-press-release.com

This website's automatic Facebook sign-in feature glitches every time I try it, and I typically have to sign in with the ID and password. There is no easy hits count on this website or on PR.com, so I can't tell if thousands or zero people have seen the releases I have created. The free sites might make the bulk of their revenues from advertising, as there are pretty large ads for Publishers Clearing House and a Free Medium Reading on my releases with them. These might distract serious journalists. The title max is 120 characters, the summary 200, and the body 5,000. Even after you sign in, the site does not remember your info, and you have to re-enter your company's name and contact information with each release. You have to choose a specific location here, as there is no world-wide option.

**PR.com**
https://www.pr.com

This is the first website I create my press releases for as it has a well organized setup system. The title has a 170 characters limit, the summary 500, and the body can be pretty lengthy. All hyperlinks are $29.95 over the free basic price. I usually just leave URL's in the release alone, as they do not automatically become paid hyperlinks. Adding an image costs $60, so I typically do not add any images here. Only one industry channel is free, and typically I choose, "Arts & Entertainment: Books" and this fits exactly what my publishing company is selling. Its free to send the release to all regions internationally, and the cost goes up if you want to focus on any narrow geographical regions. After you set up an account and log in, the site remembers your information and auto-fills the contact info. Some releases can be rejected by the Editor. One of my releases back from 2014 is still on an editorial hold because: 1. it included first or second person voices versus solely a third-person "journalistic" voice. Also, the Editor asked me to remove the sentence: "Thank you for reviewing this release from Anaphora" "as this type of information should not be in a press release." It is always a good idea to write press releases in third person. But, I still don't know why it's not a good idea to be polite and to thank viewers for reading... I recommend opening this site with Chrome because it frequently glitches with Explorer.

## PRLog.org
http://www.prlog.org

You need a business email account to setup an account with PRLog. It will not accept gmail, yahoo or other generic email accounts, as they are trying to avoid spam from anybody who cannot afford a business email address. This is the only free site that lists the exact amount of hits each release has generated. The number of hits for my last dozen press releases ranges from 182 to 778. These are pretty strong numbers, but I wish they translated into more press coverage. This is probably my favorite site not only because of the availability of statistics, but also because the inclusion of the Anaphora logo and a low-resolution image can be included in a free release. The site also bolds the title and headings, indents, and has other appealing formatting features that are added without me deliberately inserting HTML. The foreign ads are less intrusive, and the whole site has a calmer, more newsworthy feel to it.

## PRUrgent.com

http://www.prurgent.com

I only used this site once so far because the submissions page includes a warning that "due to a large number of submissions," most free releases will not be included. I believe my one release was included, so I might start submitting to them more regularly.

## OnlinePRNews.com

https://www.onlineprnews.com

This is another site I have under-used, with only two submissions, both of which were approved at the free level, which allows for 1 live URL, but only in the contact area. One unusual detail is that the release only stays live for 90 days, and only 1 submission is allowed daily. According to PRLog, some of my older releases have climbed to over 1,000 hits with time, so the expiration date is not a positive. The word limits are also shorter here, with only 100 characters for the title, and 160 for the summary.

# REVIEWERS

If you have seen similar books to yours in a Barnes and Noble, or previously bought similar titles, it's probably a good idea to mail or email a few or perhaps several review copies. Larger publishers might automatically send review copies to a few dozen or a few hundred reviewers. Smaller presses are less likely to send these release copies automatically. Writers who work with small presses, or who self-publish should take the initiative to determine which, if any, reviewers are suitable for their publication and to mail or email review copies to them.

The current Anaphora policy is that PDF review copies and press releases are sent out without any cost to the writer to my marketing list of 10,000 emails (reviewers, professors, booksellers, and the like). If a writer sends a short list of the reviewers that have published stories about them before or those in their region, I create a press release and letter to advertise the book and email just information for that single author. The general emails typically include around a dozen new releases, so that there will be something for all of the potential readers (fiction, non-fiction, poetry). Either way, I create a PDF and epub review copies that I upload to Box or DropBox and email links to these with the releases. I used to solely use Box, but then it once reached the maximum 10GB data limit in a month and got jammed, so that I had to email Box several times before they cleared the problem and reviewers could once again see the files there. If you receive angry emails from reviewers asking you why they can't see the book you sent to them via Box, this is likely to be the problem at hand. I use Microsoft's 365 Outlook program to email these releases to BCC recipients. I researched several other platforms, but this one allows for 500 email contacts per email and up to 10,000 email recipients per day, which is the volume that matches the size of my email list.

If the writer wants to send a release to one of the larger reviewers, such as *Library Journal* or *Publisher's Weekly*, which only review printed book submissions, then the writer can purchase any number of copies of their book at the regular 25% off discount and have them shipped to the publisher. Previously, I inserted the press releases, letters and a copy of the book into an envelope and shipped it out to the reviewers. About a year ago, I changed this process to one where I create a marketing version of the book cover with the LCCN, ISBN and other numbers and information that typically are added to the letter and press release on top of the biography and summary that are already usually found on the cover. Adding marketing information makes it easier for reviewers to find it and serves to replace the inserted letter/ release. This way, review copies can be shipped directly from the printer to reviewers, avoiding damage that can result from re-packaging and re-shipping. I switched after I noticed at ALA, SIBA and other book exhibit shows that I was being offered these types of galley review copies via the mail or at the exhibit tables when I was asking for books to review for my own Anaphora journals: PLJ and CCR.

If a review is published, it is likely that the book would sell more copies through online and other distribution channels than it otherwise would. The process is pretty expensive for authors, so only books that are strong enough to generate reviews (a small percentage of all releases) should be sent out. The bigger reviewers also ask for a 4-6 months delay prior to publication. So, if a writer wants their book in-print as-soon-as-possible, waiting for reviews might only delay the publication. Emailing press releases and PDF copies of the book, on the other hand, is a good idea for almost any average book, as a small note in your local paper is likely to increase local bookstore sales, and attendance at a potential book launch.

National publications only review the best out of hundreds or thousands of books that they receive. The chances that your book will be reviewed is small. You should take your marketing budget and book-quality into account when considering if you should send here. Check with each publication to see how many review copies they need; they are likely to need at least two. Submissions must be sent from 3 to 6 months prior to the date of publication.

*Include the following information with all of your books*: Author's name and title; name, address, and telephone number of publisher; date of publication; price; number of pages; and ISBN and LCCN numbers, if available. Please indicate whether any illustrations, an index, or bibliography will be included; also include a brief description of the book, its intended audience, and information on the author's background.

At the 2016 American Library Association Convention, I attended a session for private school librarians, and asked which reviewers they usually look at first when deciding on which books to buy for their libraries. One of the librarians emailed this list to me: *School Library Journal, Library Journal*, Choice, Kirkus Review, Horn Book (children/ YA), Teacher Librarian (K-12), VOYA, School Library Connection (K-12), Booklist, Book Links (K-12 literature, related to Booklist), *New York Review of Books*, as well as major newspaper book review columns and professional teaching organization journals (i.e. *History Teacher Journal*). In a follow-up question, I said that many of these charge authors for reviews. She seemed to be unfamiliar with the payment requirement, and it did not change her mind about the list. These review publications are owned by the Big Four publishers, or are operated by government-related agencies, or are for-profit enterprises that profit from author fees in exchange for reviews (which occasionally are negative despite payments). Because these are also the most "respected" reviewers by librarians, it's easy to see how the publishing industry is stacked against independent, smaller presses without a budget to pay for reviews, press coverage and the like. Still, even if you will receive a single review after sending dozens, this can be a great boost for the book and for an author's reputation.

The following listings include the publishing source, contact information and special instructions for writers. The initial list included more sources. In this list for the fifth edition, I am taking out some of the listings, and leaving only those that I usually recommend to writers that work with me.

## San Francisco Book Review

c/o City Book Review
930 Alhambra Blvd., Suite 240
Sacramento, CA 95816

*Notes*: They require 2 copies per title. I recommend this publication and their branches in other cities above the other sources because this has been the only place that has reviewed several Anaphora titles without asking for review fees. They have an online portal where you can submit ebook review copies if you do not have a budget to ship printed copies to their office.

## Midwest Book Review

Bookwatch (and other sections)
James A. Cox, Editor-in-Chief
278 Orchard Dr.
Oregon, WI 53575

*Notes*: This publication has reviewed nearly all of the books that I have sent in for review, adding up to dozens of titles. I definitely recommend them for somebody that only has a few copies to send. Send 2 printed copies with a press release after the release date. They occasionally accept emailed press releases and printed review copies separately from the printer, which is very convenient for small presses. If you want to receive a pre-release blurb from them to put on the final cover, they charge $50 to review a galley in advance of publication.

## Harper's Magazine

Suggestions for Readings Section
666 Broadway, 11th Floor
New York, NY 10012
http://harpers.org/harpers/submissions.

*Notes*: Do not mail unsolicited submissions for any section but Readings. Submissions to the Readings section are welcome at readings@

harpers.org and are encouraged, though volume precludes individual acknowledgment.

**Publisher's Weekly**
Nonfiction Reviews
[or "Poetry Reviews" or other relevant category]
71 West 23 St. #1608
New York, NY 10010

*Notes*: You now have to begin the submission process through their online publisher portal, and then you have the option to send the book electronically or to mail copies with a printed notice generated by the website. For mailed reviews, you must submit 2 books, 4 months before release date. Attach a press release with the: "Title, Author, Price, Publisher and imprint, Format, Number of pages in the finished book, 13-digit ISBN, Month and day of publication, Distribution arrangements, and Publicity contact information. An accompanying letter should contain a description or synopsis of the book, and any pertinent publicity information, including the author's previous titles, blurbs, or previous reviews." Genre: Nonfiction, Fiction, Mystery, Science Fiction/Fantasy/Horror, Romance, Poetry, Comics, and Lifestyles.

**New York Times Book Review**
Attention: Editor
620 Eighth Avenue, 5th Floor
New York, NY 10018

**Library Journal**
Attention: Book Review Editor
123 Wiliam Street, Suite 802
New York, NY 10038

*Notes*: Submit 4 months before publication. Include a press release with "Author, title; name, address, and telephone number of publisher; date of publication; price; number of pages; and ISBN and LC numbers if available. Please indicate whether any illustrations, an index, or bibliography will be included; also include a brief description of the book, its intended audience, and information on the author's background."

## Booklist
Brad Hooper, Adult Books Editor
Gillian Engberg, Books for Youth Editor
Mary Ellen Quinn, Reference Books Bulletin Editor
American Library Association
50 E. Huron
Chicago, IL 60611
Submission Information: http://www.ala.org/offices/publishing/booklist/booklist_mag/insidebooklist/booklistproc/proceduressubmitting

*Notes*: Send 2 copies. Read by most librarians. "*Book Links* articles provide comprehensive information on using books in the classroom, including thematic bibliographies with related discussion questions and activities, author and illustrator interviews and essays..."

## ForeWord Reviews
Attention: Book Review Editor
425 Boardman Ave., Suite B
Traverse City, MI 49684

*Notes*: Mail a copy of the book with a press release at least 3 months prior to the publication date. (Only 125 reviews per year). State that you are interested in the free "ForeWord Review," the other types of reviews come with $129+ prices. "Include category, title, subtitle, author, publisher, number of illustrations, pages, prices, binding, ISBNs of formats, and publication dates. Press releases or fact sheets should summarize why the title is distinctive and different; include the publisher's name, address, telephone, and fax number."

## Kirkus Reviews
*ATTN: Kirkus Indie*
*65 West 36th St., Suite 700*
*New York, N.Y. 10018*

*Notes*: Kirkus states on their website that they do not review poetry (unless it is for children), reference books, POD books, and other types of books for free. POD and small publishers as well as self-publishing authors and other groups that aren't covered with their free edition can pay $425+ for a *Kirkus Indie* review, which is guaranteed to be written, though it can be negative.

**The Horn Book, Inc.**
56 Roland Street, Suite 200
Boston, MA 02129

*Notes*: Children and teens genre only.

**Foreward Magazine**
Attention: Book Review Editor
425 Boardman Ave., Suite B
Traverse City, MI 49684

**Chicago Tribune**
Attention: Courtney Crowder
435 N. Michigan Ave.
TT 500
Chicago, IL 60611

**The Believer, McSweeney's**
*Reviews Editor*
849 Valencia Street
San Francisco, CA 94110

**Black Issues Book Review**
Attention: Susan McHenry, Editorial Director
Empire State Building
350 Fifth Avenue #1522
New York, NY 10118-0165

**Book Forum**
Attention: Book Review Editor
350 Seventh Avenue
New York, NY 10001

**BookPage**
ProMotion Inc.
2143 Belcourt Avenue

Nashville, TN 37212

**The Book Report**
Tom Donadio, Editorial Manager
250 West 57th Street #1228
New York, NY 10107

**Context**
Tim Feeney, Book Review Editor
ISU Campus 8905
Normal, IL 61790-8905

**Design Book Review**
Richard Ingersoll, Editor
Design Book Review
1418 Spring Way
Berkeley, CA 94708

**January Magazine**
#100-1001 W. Broadway #192
Vancouver, British Columbia V6H 4E4, Canada

**Lambda Book Report**
Greg Herren, Editor
Lambda Literary Foundation
P.O. Box 73910
Washington, DC 20056-3910

**Locus**
Carolyn Cushman, Senior Editor
Jonathan Strahan, Reviews Editor
Locus Publications
P.O. Box 13305
Oakland, CA 94661

**London Review of Books**
28 Little Russell
London, WC1A 2HN United Kingdom

**New Age Retailer**
Book Review Editor
119 N. Commercial Street #560
Bellingham, WA 98225

**New Yorker**
Book Review Editor
The Conde Naste Building
4 Times Square
New York, NY 10036

**Pages**
Editor-In-Chief
Creation Integrated Media
5880 Oberlin Drive
San Diego, CA 92121

**Quill & Quire**
Review Editor
St. Joseph Media
111 Queen St. East #320
Toronto, Ontario M5C 1S2, Canada

**Saturday Evening Post**
Book Review Editor
1100 Waterway Boulevard
Indianapolis, IN 46202

**Sci/Tech Book News**
Managing Editor,
5739 N.E. Sumner Street
Portland, OR 97218

**Teacher Librarian**
Book Review Editor
16211 Oxford Court
Bowie, MD 20715

**Utne Reader**
Media Reviews
12 N. 12th St., Suite 400
Minneapolis, MN 55403

**CHOICE**
575 Main St., Suite 300
Middletown, CT 06457-3445

**Boston Globe**
Book Review Editor
P.O. Box 55819
Boston, MA 02205

**Chicago Tribune Books**
435 N. Michigan Ave.
Chicago, IL 60611

**Los Angeles Review of Books**
6671 Sunset Blvd., Suite 1521
Los Angeles, CA 90028

**Los Angeles Times Book Review**
Attention: Editor Joy Press
202 West 1st Street
Los Angeles, CA 90012

**Miami Herald**
Book Reviewer
One Herald Place
Miami, FL 33132

**NPR**
Book Review Editor
1111 North Capitol St., NE
Washington, D.C. 20002

**American Book Review**
School of Arts & Sciences

University of Houston-Victoria
3007 N. Ben Wilson
Victoria, TX 77901

**Philadelphia Inquirer**
Book Review Editor
PO Box 8263
Philadelphia, PA 19101

**Independent**
Book Review Editor
2 Derry Street
London W8 5HF
United Kingdom

**Guardian and Observer**
Book Reviews Editor
Kings Place, 90 York Way
London N1 9GU
4420-3-353-2000

**Spectator**
Book Reviews Editor
22 Old Queen Street
London
SW1H 9HP
01795-592886

**New Statesman**
Book Reviews Editor
John Carpenter House
7 Carmelite Street
Blackfriars
London
EC4Y 0BS
44-0-20-7936-6400

**Daily Post-Athenian**
Book Reviews Editor

PO Box 340
Athens TN, 37371-0340
423-745-5664

**Augusta Chronicle**
Book Reviews Editor
725 Broad Street
Augusta, GA 30901
706-724-0851

**VOYA Magazine**
Reviews Editor
16211 Oxford CT
Bowie, MD 20715

**Colorado Review**
9105 Campus Delivery
Department of English
Colorado State University
Fort Copllins, CO 80523-910

**Gulf Coast**
Department of English
University of Houston
Houston, TX 77204-3013

**New Orleans Review**
Loyola University
Box 195
Ndew Ortleans, LA 70118

**The Nation**
33 Irving Place
New York, N.Y. 10003

**The Seattle Times**
1000 Denny Way
Seattle, WA 98109

**Rattle**
122411 Ventura Boulevard
Studio City, CA 91604

**Salt Lake Tribune**
Attn: Book Review Editor
90 So. 400 West
Salt Lake City, UT 84101

**San Diego Union Tribune**
John Wilkens, Book Writer
P.O. Box 120191
San Diego, CA 92112

**Slate**
Attn: Book Review Editor
95 Morton Street, 4th Floor
New York, NY 10014

**London Review of Books**
28 Little Russell Street
London WC1A 2HN

Include a SASE if you do not use email. Review copies should be sent for the attention of the editors at the above address. "Unfortunately we can't return books we decide not to review."

**The Albuquerque Journal**
David Steinberg, Books Editor
The Albuquerque Journal
7777 Jefferson Street
NE, Albuquerque, NM 07109

**Arizona Daily Star**
J.C. Martin
PO Box 65388
Tucson AZ 85728-5388

**The Arizona Republic**
Dan Kincaid, Book Editor
200 E Van Buren
Phoenix, AZ 85004

**Austin American Statesman**
Jody Seaborn, and Joe Gross, Editors
305 S. Congress Avenue
P.O. Box 670
Austin, TX 78767

**Baltimore Sun**
501 N Calvert Street
P.O. Box 1377
Baltimore, MD 21278

**The Baton Rouge Advocate**
Books Editor
7290 Blue Bonnet Road
P.O. Box 588
Baton Rouge, LA 70821-0588

**Boston Herald**
Book Editor
1 Herald Street
P.O. Box 55843
Boston, MA 02205

**Buffalo News**
Book Review Editor
Gusto, One News Plaza
P.O. Box 100
Buffalo, NY 14240

**Charlotte Observer**
Editor, Living/Entertainment/News
600 S. Tryon Street
Charlotte, NC 28202

**Chicago Sun-Times**
Book Editor
350 N. Orleans Street, 10th Floor
Chicago, IL 60654

**Contra Costa Times**
Book Editor, Bookends
2640 Shadelands Drive
Walnut Creek, CA 94598

**Dallas Morning News**
Assistant Arts Editor, Books
Dallas Morning News
508 Young Street
Dallas, TX 75202

**The Denver Post**
Books Editor
101 Colfax Avenue #600
Denver, CO 80202

**Detroit Free Press**
Entertainment Editor
615 West Lafayette Street
Detroit, MI 48231

**Fort Worth Star-Telegram**
400 West 7th Street
PO Box 1870
Fort Worth, TX 76115

**Hartford Courant**
Arts Editor
285 Broad Street
Hartford, CT 06115

**Houston Chronicle**
Book Editor
801 Texas Street

P.O. Box 4260
Houston, TX 77002-2904

**Indianapolis Star**
Arts & Entertainment Editor
307 N. Pennsylvania Street
Indianapolis, IN 46204

**Kansas City Star**
Arts Editor
1729 Grand Boulevard
Kansas City, MO 64108

**Louisville Courier-Journal**
Book Editor
525 W Broadway
PO Box 740031
Louisville, KY 40201-7431

**Miami Herald**
Book Editor
One Herald Plaza
Miami, FL 33132-1693

**Milwaukee Journal Sentinel**
333 W. State Street
P.O. Box 371
Milwaukee, WI 53201

**Minneapolis Star Tribune**
Books Editor
425 Portland Avenue South
Minneapolis, MN 55488

**Nashville Tennessean**
1100 Broadway
Nashville TN 37203

**Newark Star-Ledger**
Books Editor
1 Star Ledger Plaza
Newark, NJ 07102

**New Orleans Times-Picayune**
3800 Howard Avenue
New Orleans, LA 70125-1429

**Newsday**
Books Editor
235 Pinelawn Road
Melville NY 11747-4250

**New York Daily News**
Book Editor
450 West 33rd Street
New York, NY 10001

**New York Observer**
915 Broadway, 9th Floor
New York, NY 10010

**New York Post**
1211 Avenue of the Americas
New York, NY 10036

**The Oregonian**
Book Editor
1320 S.W. Broadway
Portland, OR 97201-9911

**Orlando Sentinel**
Arts and Entertainment Editor, Books
633 N. Orange Avenue
Orlando, FL 32801

**Pittsburgh Post-Gazette**
Book Editor

34 Boulevard of the Allies
PO Box 566
Pittsburgh, PA 15230

**Pittsburgh Tribune Review**
Books Editor and Features Reporter
D. L. Clark Building
503 Martindale Street, 3rd Floor
Pittsburgh, PA 15212

**The Plain Dealer**
Books Editor
Plain Dealer Plaza
1801 Superior Ave.
Cleveland, Ohio 44114

**Providence Journal-Bulletin**
Books and Travel Editor
75 Fountain Street
Providence, RI 02902

**Saint Louis Post-Dispatch**
Book Review Editor
Saint Louis Post-Dispatch
900 N. Tucker Boulevard
Saint Louis, MO 63101

**Saint Petersburg Times**
Book Editor
490 First Avenue S
P.O. Box 1121
Saint Petersburg, FL 33731

**San Antonio Express-News**
Books Editor
301 Avenue E
P.O. Box 2171
San Antonio, TX 78297-2171

**San Diego Union-Tribune**
Books Editor
PO Box 120191
San Diego, CA 92112-0191

**San Francisco Chronicle**
Book Editor
901 Mission Street
San Francisco, CA 94103

**San Jose Mercury News**
750 Ridder Park Drive
San Jose, CA 95190

**Santa Fe New Mexican**
Editor
202 E. Marcy Street
P.O. Box 2048
Santa Fe, NM 87504-2048

**Tampa Tribune**
Book Editor
The News Center
202 S. Parker Street
P.O. Box 191
Tampa, FL 33601-0191

**Toronto Star**
Book Columnist
One Yonge Street
Toronto, Ontario
M5E 1E6 Canada

*The Tucson Weekly*
Arts Editor
PO Box 27087
Tucson, AZ 85726-7087

**USA Today**
Book Review Editor
7950 Jones Branch Drive
McLean, VA 22108

**Village Voice**
Voice Literary Supplement
Senior Associate Editor
36 Cooper Square
New York, NY 1003-4846

**Wall Street Journal**
1211 Avenue of the Americas
New York, NY 10036

**Washington Post**
Book Review Editor
Ron Charles, Fiction Editor
1150 15th Street N.W.
Washington, DC 20071

**Washington Times**
Books Editor
3600 New York Avenue NE
Washington, DC 20002-1947

**Stevo's Book Reviews on the Internet**
Stevo Brock
*Email queries about reviews to*: stevo@mzinga.com
http://forums.delphiforums.com/stevo1/start

**The Akron Beacon Journal**
Book Reviews Editor
44 East Exchange Street
Akron, OH 44308

**Boston Area Small Press and Poetry Scene**
Individual Reviewer
25 School St.

Somerville, MA 02143

**Shelf Unbound**
1526 Kings Hwy.
Dallas, TX 75208

"E-mail a high res image of the book cover, author image, press release, brief author bio, and information about excerpt rights (preferably up to 10 images and/or 1,500 words) to edit@shelfmediagroup.com. If the book is available in pdf form, please submit a copy of the pdf or mail a review copy of the book."

**The Times of Northwest Indiana**
601 W. 45th Ave.
Munster, IN 46321

**Association of Writers & Writing Programs**
George Mason University
Director of Publications/Editor
Mail Stop 1E3
Fairfax, VA 22030

**The Bloomsbury Review**
1553 Platte Street, Suite 206
Denver, CO 80202-1167

**BookReview.com**
136 Owen Road
Monona, WI 53716

**Chicago Reader**
Managing Editor
11 E. Illinois
Chicago, IL 60611

**Feathered Quill Book Reviews**
info@featheredquill.com

*Notes*: Include "Free Book Review Query" in the subject line of your email, Also include a press release detailing the book and its genre. They will contact you if they have decided to give it a review.

**Independent Publisher**
Jim Barnes, Award Director, Independent Publisher
http://www.independentpublisher.com/reviews.php
jimb@bookpublishing.com

**MidAmerica**
Marcia Noe, Editor
535 Elinor St.
Chattanooga, TN 37405

*Note*: This publication discusses only Midwestern literature and art.

**Ohioana Library Association**
Ohioana Library and Book Festival
274 E. First Ave., Ste. 300
Columbus, OH 43201

**The Plain Dealer**
Book Editor
Plain Dealer Plaza
1801 Superior Avenue
Cleveland, OH 44114-2198

**Rain Taxi**
PO Box 3840
Minneapolis, MN 55403

**Redivider Journal**
Department of Writing, Literature, and Publishing
Emerson College
120 Boylston Street
Boston, MA 02116
http://www.redividerjournal.org/submit/

**RT Book Reviews**
Giselle Hirtenfeld/Goldfeder

55 Bergen Street
Brooklyn, NY 11201
Giselle@RTBookReviews.com
http://www.rtbookreviews.com/magazine/print-advertising-rates
http://www.rtbookreviews.com/
No poetry reviews.

*Note*: "If your book is very recently published, and you would like to
have it considered for one of our few web exclusive review spots, please
contact Morgan Doremus (Morgan@RTBookReviews.com), our web
editor, with your query."

**Small Press Review**
Dustbooks
P.O. Box 100
Paradise, CA 95967
Phone: 530-877-6110
Fax: 530-877-0222
info@dustbooks.com
http://www.dustbooks.com/sprguide.htm

*Notes*: "Reviews written for SPR should be 100-300 words in length.
Anything longer may be edited down, delayed in publication, or returned. Reviews near 150 words tend to be published more quickly
because they are more flexible to work with... For books [include]: author, publisher and address, price, date, type of cover (paper or cloth)
and number of pages."

**Tennessee Libraries**
Kathy Campbell, Book Reviews Editor
423-439-5629
East Tennessee State University
Box 70665
Johnson City, TN 37601
campbeka@etsu.edu

**Tuscan Weekly**
Margaret Regan, Arts Editor
The Tucson Weekly

PO Box 27087
Tucson, AZ 85726-7087

**Feminist Formations**
femform@umn.edu
http://feministformations.arizona.edu/book_reviews.html

"Feminist Formations cultivates a forum where feminists from around the world articulate research, theory, activism, teaching, and learning, thereby showcasing new feminist formations... Our subject matter includes national, global, and transnational feminist thought and practice; the cultural and social politics of genders and sexualities; and historical and contemporary studies of gendered experience."

**Her Circle: A Magazine of Women's Creative Arts and Activism**
http://www.hercircleezine.com/submission-guidelines/
books@hercircleezine.com

"We welcome well-written reviews of women's socially engaged Fiction, Creative Non-fiction, Poetry, Criticism, and Artist's Books published within the past 12 months. Please, include a jpeg image of the book cover. Word count: 500 – 800 words. Send queries or full submissions to books@hercircleezine.com."

**HerStoria Magazine**
http://www.herstoria.com/about.html
bookreviews@herstoria.com
editor@herstoria.com

*Note*: Can submit books for review as well as book reviews.

**Focuses on women's history**
Dr. Amber Kinser, Individual Reviewer
Chair, Department of Communication
East Tennessee State University
http://www.amberkinser.com
KINSERA@mail.etsu.edu
*Note*: Researches "…human Interaction in close relationships, families, and gender." Reviews academic-related material.

Jane Squires, Individual Reviewer
jrs362@hotmail.com
*Note*: Mostly reviews women authors and uplifting stories.

## Melusine, or Woman in the 21st Century
http://www.melusine21cent.com/mag/submit
sub2melusine@gmail.com

*Notes*: Online journal of literature and art "by women (but not only women) about women (and just about everything else.)." Not currently accepting book review queries due to backlog, though they'll still accept review submissions.

## Ms. Magazine
Jessica Stites, Associate Editor
jstites@msmagazine.com

## National Women's Book Association
Becky Foust
PO Box 399
Ross, CA 94957

## National Women's Studies Association
Authors Meets Critics
valda.lewis@nwsa.org
7100 Baltimore Avenue, Suite 203
College Park, MD  20740
Phone: (301) 403-0407
Fax: (301) 403-4137
Email: nwsaoffice@nwsa.org

"Authors Meet Critics sessions are designed to bring authors of recent, cutting-edge books, deemed to be important contributions to the field of women's studies, together with discussants chosen to provide a variety of viewpoints."

## Praxis: Gender and Culture Critiques
Caridad Souza, Praxis Book Review Editor
Africana-Latino Studies & Women's and Gender, Studies, SUNY

Oneonta.
http://www.oneonta.edu/academics/praxis/
Praxis@oneonta.edu

*Note*: Must be in Chicago Style.

## Seeding the Snow

LeAnn Spencer and Erin Tuttle, Editors
c/o The Conservation Foundation
10S404 Knoch Knolls Road
Naperville, Illinois 60565
submissions@SeedingtheSnow.net

*Note*: Books should be connected to a passion for the natural world.

## Society for the Study of American Women Writers

ssaww-l@mailman.ucsd.edu

*Note*: "For materials to be posted to the web site or included in the newsletter, contact Donna Campbell, Vice President for Publications, at campbelld@wsu.edu or ssaww.web@gmail.com."

## Story Circle Book Reviews

http://www.storycirclebookreviews.org/frmbookquery.shtml
Judy Miller, Editor and Reviewer
http://www.storycirclebookreviews.org/reviewers/miller.shtml
intlmom@sbcglobal.net

*Submission requirement*: Enter an ISBN number, and a link to an Amazon.com page of your book, on the submission form.

## WE Magazine for Women

Heidi Richards Mooney, Publisher
P.O. Box 550856
Fort Lauderdale, FL 33355-0856
Heidi@wemagazineforwomen.com
http://wemagazineforwomen.com/about/book-reviews/

*Notes*: *For Book Reviews*: "Please include a cover sheet or return address

so we can acknowledge we have received the book. Some of our authors include a self-addressed postcard. This is a great way to get a quicker response from our editorial team. Also be sure to include where/how to purchase and an email address so we can let you know when the book will be either listed or reviewed... Books can be autographed."
*For Author Self-Interviews*: "send us either an excerpt of the book (350 to 600 words) or an "interview" which should include why the book was written, what the book is about, etc. The author comes up with the questions and answers them... Send at least four (4) Q & A to Heidi@ wemagazineforwomen.com. Include a link to the cover of the book and a link to the author's photo. Please, no attachments. All emails with attachments will be discarded and you will not receive a reply. Be sure to send a copy of your book via mail. Book excerpts and interviews will not be posted until we actually receive a hard copy of the book."

**Woman's Era Magazine**
http://www.womansera.com/wemag/we.aspx?show=ABOUTUS
admin@womansera.com

**Women in the Arts Quarterly Journal**
wia@umsl.edu

**Women's Review of Books**
Amy Hoffman, Editor-in-Chief
Wellesley Centers for Women CHE
Wellesley College
106 Central Street
Wellesley, MA 02481

**Women's Studies: An Interdisciplinary Journal**
Kathryn Wolford, Book Review Editor
Claremont Graduate University
Department of English, Blaisdell House
143 East Tenth Street
Claremont, CA 91711

**Women Writers E-Journal**
kimwells@womenwriters.net

Dr. Natasha Whitton
Book Reviews Editor/Co-Editor
www.womenwriters.net
nwhitton@selu.edu

## BOOKSTORES AND EVENTS

While it's great to be reviewed, sometimes direct sales during readings and events can be more immediately profitable, if the event is properly publicized. Even at a small bookstore, a writer can sell 40+ copies of their book at one event. However, if you don't live in the area where the event will be held, and there is no press about the meeting, attendance can be extremely low. Therefore, it's a good idea to begin your book-reading tour in your local bookstores. Invite your friends, co-workers, family, and anybody else you know that might be interested in reading something you wrote. They will probably want to buy a copy after hearing you read from it, and most will probably feel that an autographed copy purchased during a reading adds value to the book. Workshops and festivals can also be a great way to meet new publishers, and to network within the publishing industry. Some festivals and workshops even pay writers to give lectures, speeches, or creative workshops. It's a good idea to attempt contacting a few dozen bookstores, festivals or workshops to determine if it is a beneficial route for you to take. The locations that previously invited Anaphora writers are likely to do so in the future. These are also more likely to invite writers from other small presses.

### ANAPHORA WRITERS PREVIOUSLY READ AT

\* = Larger events.

**Poetry Library at The Last Tuesday Society**
London, England

www.poetrylibrary.org.uk.

Has poetry readings, such as open-mic nights, writing groups, and courses.

**\*The International Poetry Festival**
Swansea, Wales
www.peterthabitjones.com

A three-day festival of poetry readings, book and art portfolio displays, and more.

**Mt. Sac Writer's Weekend**
Walnut, CA
http://www.mtsac.edu/instruction/humanities/elj/events/weekend/index.html

Holds writing programs, workshops, an open-mic, and writers' day prizes. This writer's weekend is geared toward fiction, creative non-fiction, and poetry writers.

**Small World Books**
Venice Beach, CA
http://www.smallworldbooks.com/.

**\*Tebot Bach Huntington**
Beach, CA
www.tebotbach.org

Provides writing workshops and book readings for poets specifically.

**Learning Communities Series**
Middle Georgia College
http://www.mgc.edu/reading/lc/

Readings, festivals, and other events are held at this college.

**First Tuesdays with the Writers' Roundtable**
Newton, NJ

http://www.jeanleblancpoetry.com/the-writers-roundtable.htm

Has readings that occur the first Tuesday of almost every month and are open to poets and prose writers.

## The Carriage House Poetry Series
Fanwood, NJ
http://carriagehousepoetryseries.blogspot.com/

Have been known to feature both nationally-known and local poets. Readings are held on the third Tuesday of almost every month.

## Florida Library's Poetry Café
Florida, NY
http://poetry.openmikes.org/listings/floridalibraryspoetrycafe

Holds a poetry open mic night on the second Thursday of every month.

## 2nd April Galerie & Studios
Canton, OH
www.secondapril.org

Has put on book signings, as well as "Canton's First Friday Poetry Spectacular", which is an event that takes place on the first Friday of every month. This show includes a featured poet, open mic, and poetry slam with cash prizes for the winners.

## Spoken Word Festival
Theater of the Seventh Sister Lancaster, PA
http://seventhsister.com/?p=127

A three-day event filled with storytelling and stage poetry. General Admission is $15.

## The Lancaster Poetry Exchange
Lancaster, PA
www.lancasterpoetry.com

Offers poetry readings, book signings, and writer's workshops.

## The Wise Owl Bookstore
West Reading, PA
www.wiseowlbookstore.com

Offers events such as "Poetry & Coffee", open mic nights, and other author events.

## Bookmans Entertainment Exchange
Tucson, Arizona
www.bookmans.com

This bookstore focuses on selling used books, games, electronics, musical instruments, and more. While this location doesn't focus on books specifically, an Anaphora writer has had a book signing here and they are friendly to a wide variety of entertainment.

## Mostly Books
Tucson, AZ
www.mostlybooksaz.com

This independent bookstore holds events such as Local Author Open House, book signings, and discussion groups for all sorts of genres.

## Barnes & Noble Birdcage Walk
Citrus Heights, CA
http://store-locator.barnesandnoble.com/store/2885

Has regular author events, such as readings and book signings. This location is especially friendly to authors who write fiction and children's books.

## Book Carnival
Orange, CA
www.annesbookcarnival.com

This store offers book readings and book signings for mystery and romantic suspense writers.

**Gatsby Books**
Long Beach, CA
www.gatsbybooks.com

Has everything from Meet the Author events to book readings to book signings, which is friendly to all genres and writers.

**The Laguna Beach Public Library**
Laguna Beach, CA
http://web.ocpl.org/events/?b=Laguna%20Beach

Schedules book signings, book discussions, and writing contests for all genres.

**The Village Bookshop**
Glendora, CA
www.villagebookshopglendora.com

Has visiting writers' readings, writing groups, and other events geared to all genres.

**Charis Books**
Atlanta, GA
http://www.charisbooksandmore.com/.
This independent bookstore specializes in unique children's books, feminist and cultural studies books, as well as queer fiction and non-fiction.

**Kazoo Books**
Kalamazoo, MI
http://www.kazoobooks.com/

Has book readings (local and visiting), book discussion groups, and other events geared to all genres.

**The Fine Grind Coffee Bar**
Little Falls, NJ
http://www.thefinegrindcoffeebar.com/

ANNA FAKTOROVICH

Has book signings, free writing seminars, and open mic nights every Sunday.

**Hudson Library**
Hudson, OH
http://www.hudsonlibrary.org/Events/Adult%20Flyers/OhioAuthor-Day.html

This library offers book sales, readings with featured authors, and an annual book fair that is friendly to a wide variety of genres.

**Marietta Day Annual Festival**
Marietta, PA
http://mariettapa.com/MariettaDay/2001.html
To reserve your space, visit: http://www.mariettapabusiness.com/_images/MARIETTA_DAY_Vendor.pdf.

This is not a book festival, but there have been book signings at this event. To be a vendor, you must reserve your space and the cost is $35 for a 20X10 foot area.

**Tamarack**
Beckley, WV
www.tamarackwv.com

This shopping area is "The Best of West Virginia" with not only artisan demonstrations and food tastings, but Meet the Author events and book signings as well.

**Taylor Books**
Charleston, WV
www.taylorbooks.com

This independent bookstore has events ranging from book signings to lectures to art classes.

**West Virginia Book Festival**
Charleston, WV

wvbookfestival.org

This two-day event offers book vendors, the Festival Marketplace, a special section just for children, a used book sale, meet the author events, workshops, and panel discussions.

## OTHER BOOKSTORES AND EVENTS

\* = Larger events that are more inclined to sell your books, but may be more difficult to get in.

*For more poetry locations, check*:
http://www.poets.org/page.php/prmID/382

**\*Tucson Festival of Books**
University of Arizona
Tucson, Arizona
www.tucsonfestivalofbooks.org

**\*Beyond Baroque**
Venice, CA
www.beyondbaroque.org

This location is very friendly to poets. They offer open, public readings and an annual Beyond Baroque Poetry Contest where the 1st place winner receives $1000!

**Marin Poetry Center**
Falkirk Cultural Center
San Rafael, CA
www.marinpoetrycenter.org

This program welcomes anyone who is interested in the art of spoken word.

**Santa Cruz Poetry**
Santa Cruz, CA

http://www.baymoon.com/~poetrysantacruz/index.html.

**The Poetry Center**
San Francisco State University
http://www.sfsu.edu/~poetry/

Holds about five poetry readings per month, and also gives out awards to poets.

**Colorado Poets Center**
Greeley, CO
www.coloradopoetscenter.org

**\*Palm Beach Poetry Festival**
Palm Beach, FL
www.palmbeachpoetryfestival.org

This festival has evening readings and performances, afternoon talks, and a panel discussion by some of America's most award-winning poets.

**Highland Park Poetry**
Highland Park, IL
www.highlandparkpoetry.org

Offers readings, open mic nights, workshops, and contests for poets.

**The Poetry Center of Chicago**
Chicago, IL
www.poetrycenter.org

Features readings, contests, and workshops ranging from beginners to masters.

**\*Poetry Foundation**
Chicago, IL
www.poetryfoundation.org

This foundation has events ranging from Poetry Out Loud to readings and lectures, including Poetry conversations.

## New Orleans Literary Festival
New Orleans, LA
www.tennesseewilliams.net

This festival features a wide variety of authors, has literary panel discussions, and a Literary Late Night series. While the festival takes place in March, there are other events throughout the year such as Coffee and Conversation in the fall.

**New Jersey**: Go to http://njpoetspoetry.blogspot.com/ for updates on upcoming poetry readings and events in New Jersey.

## *Poets House
Manhattan, NY
www.poetshouse.org

Sponsors festivals, readings, workshops, and other events such as the Poetry walk across the Brooklyn Bridge.

## *Poetry Society of America
New York, NY
www.poetrysociety.org.

Offers awards, readings, and also sponsors a variety of national events such as Red, White, & Blue: Poets on Politics.

## The Downtown Writers' Center
Syracuse, NY
www.ymcaofgreatersyracuse.org.

Features awards, creative writing workshops, visiting author reading series.

## Cleveland State University Poetry Center
Cleveland, OH
http://www.csuohio.edu/poetrycenter/

Holds reading series and contests for poets.

**Imagination**
Cleveland, OH
http://www.csuohio.edu/class/imagination/

This conference offers readings by workshop and guest faculty, conferences, receptions, and social gatherings.

**\*The Kenyon Review Literary Festival**
Gambier, OH
http://www.kenyonreview.org/programs/literary-festival/

"Every fall, The Kenyon Review at Kenyon College presents a celebration of literature featuring readings by local, national, and international authors, workshops, presentations, and more."

**Visible Voice Books**
Cleveland, OH
info@visiblevoicebooks.com
1023 Kenilworth
Cleveland, Ohio 44113
Phone: 216-961-0084
Fax: 216-615-7571
http://www.visiblevoicebooks.com/

Hosts special events at the store, including author visits and signings, events in conjunction with the monthly Tremont Art Walk, and readings by local authors and open mic poetry evenings.

**Silverton Poetry Festival**
Silverton, OR
www.silvertonpoetry.org

This festival features open mic nights and sponsors poetry readings, workshops, publications, and other events.

**The Ohio River Festival of Books**
Huntington, WV
www.ohioriverbooks.org

Holds open mic poetry events, author signings, and readings for a variety of ages. This festival typically takes place in April over the course of a week.

**West Virginia Writers, Inc.**
www.wvwriters.org

This group supports writers and poets in the state and beyond with an annual conference, regional workshops, writing competitions, an online writers' roundtable, event and opportunity listings, and more.

**Home Days on the Green**
Broadview Heights, OH
Annette Phelps, Promotional Booth Representative
APhelps@broadview-heights.org

**Ohioana Book Festival**
Ohioana Library
Linda Hengst, Executive Director
LHENGST@ohioana.org
http://www.ohioanabookfestival.org/

Presents the annual Ohioana Book Festival celebrating Ohio's authors

## LIBRARIES

If you thought that a reviewer is likely to review your book, it is also likely that there is one or more library that wants to buy your book. Library book purchases have gone down slightly in the recent years due to budget-cuts in the cultural sector, but most libraries are still actively buying a great deal of books. It's a good idea to attempt selling to local libraries first, especially if they are familiar with you as a customer. An acquisition librarian might buy more than one book, so the effort might be worth-while. Anaphora works with Coutts Information Services, a branch of Ingram, with its library distribution services. But, Coutts only distributes a few of the strongest Anaphora titles, and Coutts only sells them to the top academic libraries in the U.S. So, it's a good idea for all writers to make a few phone calls to acquisition librarians to make a few sales. It is likely that if a writer finds a local library to buy their book, that same library will buy future Anaphora titles, which would increase automatic library sales through Coutts and other distribution methods. There are thousands of libraries in the US, and calling each of them with each new title would do more to annoy the acquisition librarians than sell more books. The approach of having writers contact a few libraries that fit their title is more likely to generate overall results. A full-time marketing and sales staff is also needed for an effort like this.

Several writers have asked me about my marketing policies. There is a pretty long answer to this question, and I'll attempt answering it here with the shortest means possible. A single successful marketer is likely to make a minimum of $60,000 in salary, health-insurance and other costs. Only small presses with revenues over $200,000 can afford hiring more than 1 full-time employee. And if a small press has one full-time employee, he or she has to select titles, proofread, edit, design, format, publish titles, do annual and quarterly taxes, keep accounts, and a very long list of other tasks. If a small press, such as Anaphora, publishes 30 titles per year, and attempts calling 3,000 librarians for every title, it would have to make 90,000 phone calls per year, each of which would take 15 minutes to be mildly successful, for a total of 1,350,000 minutes, or 22,500 hours per year, or 61 hours per day of library calling... Er, well, I think that one person can't work 61 hours in a 24 hour period. So, a staff of at least 8 full-time marketers working 8-hour days is needed to fully market 30 book titles per year. These 8 marketers would make $480,000. How many books can these marketers sell? Each of the 30 titles has to make $16,000 in profits just to cover the marketers' salaries. Calculate in that these books better have the most brilliant design and editing, and you need a staff of 8 editors, designers, accountants and a lawyer (one should be enough, but he'll cost $300,000). Basically, you have to make a minimum of $40,000 per title for this to work. You might have noticed that we are now talking about minimum revenue of $1,200,000 per year. Well, how exactly would this entity be a "small" publisher? So, if a writer wants a "marketing budget," they should write popular fiction, and seek one of the top 10 publishers in the US, as only they have enough incoming revenue to afford a marketing budget. Everybody else has to come up with innovative marketing approaches that save money, and leave more profits both for the writer and for the publisher.

**Queens University Library**
jonesw@queensu.ca

**University of Arizona**
terry.lawler@phoenix.gov

**California State**
mgerman@exchange.calstatela.edu

**Hayward Campus Library**
aline.soules@csueastbay.edu

**California State University, Sacramento**
keysm@library.csus.edu

**Chapman University**
russo@chapman.ed

**Claremont College**
Lisa_Crane@cuc.claremont.edu

**Monterey County Public Library**
PagetRL@co.monterey.ca.us
Children's Librarian

**San Jose State University**
Mary.Nino@sjsu.edu

**Sonoma State University**
karen.brodsky@sonoma.edu

**University of Florida**
floturc@uflib.ufl.edu

**Chattahoocee Valley Library**
rshader@cvrls.net

**Mercer University Library**
TIMMS_GP@mercer.edu

**University of Columbus**
eadill@iupuc.edu

**Idaho State University**
kourregi@isu.edu

**Eastern Illinois University Library**
jmderr@eiu.edu

**Garret**
Evangelical Theological Seminary
beth.sheppard@garrett.edu

**Illinois State Library**
mbruns1@ilstu.edu
VANDELLABROWN@aol.com
Diversity Consultant at the Library and is also an Author/ Illustrator

**Northern Illinois University Library**
wfinley@niu.edu

**Oak Lawn Public Library**
jcasey@olpl.org
Director

**University of Illinois, Urbana**
mkschnei@illinois.edu

**Warren Newport Public Library**

dstine@wnpl.info

**Bloomfield Eastern Green County Library**
Indianapolis, IN
jhelling@bloomfield.lib.in.us
Director

**Indiana State University**
sfrey@isugw.indstate.ed

**Notre Dame**
FSMITH3@ND.EDU

**Purdue University**
cfriehle@purdue.edu

**Iowa Library Services**
maryannmori@aol.com
District Library Consultant

**Iowa State University**
spassonn@iastate.edu

**Greater Kansas City Association of School Libraries**
Kris.Baughman@raytownschools.org

**South Central Kansas Library**
tom@sckls.info

**Campbellsville University**
jrburch@campbellsville.edu

**St. Catherine's University**
EJAsch@stkate.edu

**Western Kentucky University**
Roxanne.Spencer@wku.edu

**Louisiana State University**

skelsey@lsu.edu

## School of Library and Information Science
mmck@lsu.edu

## Maryland State
gshirley@msde.state.md.us
Library Coordinator for the State of Maryland

## Central Michigan University
maths1sm@cmich.edu
matyn1mj@cmich.edu

## Genesee District Library
CHeron@thegdl.org

## Michigan State University
flynnhol@mail.lib.msu.edu

## Wayne State University
aa3805@wayne.edu
dcharbon@med.wayne.edu

## Western Michigan University
sharon.carlson@wmich.edu

## Red Wing
james.lund@ci.red-wing.mn.us
Library Director

## Metropolitan Community College, Maple Woods
Kansas City
mwnorthrup@kc.rr.com
Has written on publishing and also reviews children's books

## University of Central Missouri
ruleman@libserv.ucmo.edu

## Webster Groves Public Library

tcooper@wgpl.or

*Note:* Also a part of the Mid-American Library Alliance.

**University of Nevada**
ragains@unr.edu
Business and Government Librarian

**Bernalillo County Library System**
kbarco@cabq.gov

**Carlsbad Public Library**
bnieman@elinlib.org

**New Mexico Library Association**
valnye@gmail.com
Secretary

**Mid-America Baptist Theological Seminary**
jimancuso@mabtsne.edu

**Lehman College**
janet.munch@lehman.cuny.edu

**Queens Library**
Queens Borough
Ellen.Mehling@queenslibrary.org
Mark.T.Donnelly@queenslibrary.org

**Appalachian State University Library**
donovangl@appstate.edu
johnsnkw@appstate.edu
farisonll@appstate.edu
johnsnkw@appstate.edu

**Public Library of Charlotte and Mecklenurg County**
maleonard@plcmc.org

**University of North Carolina, Greensboro**

alwhite@uncg.edu

## University of North Carolina, Charlotte
Lisa.Nickel@uncc.edu
lstickel@uncc.edu

## Bowling Green State University
gevans@bgsu.edu

## Cleveland State University
Special Collections Librarian
clevelandmemory@yahoo.com

## Cuyahoga Public Library
Parma, OH
BWLODARCZAK@cuyahogalibrary.org

## Kent State
jharri18@kent.edu

*Note*: Editor at the Kent State University Press.

## Kent State Library
jseeholz@kent.edu

## Mentor Public Library
Lynn.Hawkins@mentorpl.or
Library Director

## Ohioana Library
LHENGST@ohioana.org
Director of Library. Also in charge of organizing the Ohioana Book Festival.

## University of Akron
jfranks@uakron.edu

## Oregon Institute of Technology
dawn.lowewincentsen@oit.edu

**Bloomsburg University Library**
kyelinek@bloomu.edu

**Whitehall Public Library**
Pittsburgh
lslimon@yahoo.com

**Providence College**
ebailey@providence.edu

**University of South Carolina**
KINGDP1@mailbox.sc.edu

**Denton Library** (TX)
Kimberly.Wells@cityofdenton.com
Public Service Librarian

**Texas A&M University, Kingsville**
kabrs00@tamuk.edu

**Texas State University**
es02@txstate.edu

**University of North Texas**
Erin.OToole@unt.edu

**University of Texas, Austin**
loriene@ischool.utexas.edu
President of the American Library Association in 2007-2008

**University of Texas, Kingsville**
victoria.packard@tamuk.edu
Coordinator of Instructional Services and Distance Learning

**Utah State University**
erin.davis@usu.edu

**Fletcher Free Library** (Burlington)
bshatara@ci.Burlington.vt.us
Outreach and Reference Librarian

**Virginia Commonwealth University**
jglover2@vcu.edu

**Central Washington University**
brittom@cwu.EDU

**Western Washington University**
Elizabeth.Stephan@wwu.edu

# DEVELOPING A CONTACTS LIST

There is turn-around among librarians, bookstore managers and review editors, so you are likely to discover that a few of the email addresses in this book will be out of date. So, it is a good idea for every writer to come up with their own contacts list that covers the reviewers and book buyers that are relevant for your book and for your geographic region. Here are a few websites that will help you to run searches for the best contacts for you:

**Newspaper Lists:**
http://www.50states.com/news/#.U5fK_3VGTIU

**Review Publications List:**
http://www.newpages.com/npguides/reviews.htm

**Columnists:**
http://www.blueagle.com/

**List of Conferences:**
http://writing.shawguides.com/

**20 Top Book Clubs Operated by:**

http://bookspan.com/contact/

**Websites for Promoting EBooks:**
http://www.mediabistro.com/galleycat/free-ebook-promotion_b52130

**Readings, Fairs and Festivals**
www.bookweb.org; www.booksense.com; www.booksamillion.com, www.readings.org

**Libraries Lists:**
www.publiclibraries.com; www.nlc-bnc.ca/canlib/epublic.htm; http://www.ala.org/tools/libfactsheets/alalibraryfactsheet22; http://librarytechnology.org/libraries; http://www.lib-web.org;

**Bookstore Directories:**
www.newenglandbooks.org; www.booksense.com; www.bookweb.org

**Amazon Top Reviewers (begin with #50 as the top ones are busy):**
http://www.amazon.com/review/top-reviewers

**List of Awards for Different Genres:**
https://www.goodreads.com/award

**Notable or Free to Apply Awards to Consider:**
*James Tait Black Prizes:* There are no application forms to complete. Submissions for both the book and drama prizes should be sent to the Department of English Literature:
The James Tait Black Prizes
English Literature
School of Literatures, Languages and Cultures
The University of Edinburgh
50 George Square
Edinburgh
EH8 9LH

*SFWA Awards:* Only for science fiction and fantasy. Send email to webeditor@sfwa.org asking for permission to offer free complimentary copies of your book to any SFWA member that is interested in reviewing it for the SFWA awards. Also ask for a listing for the title in the Nebula Awards Report with an annotation about the offer of a complimentary copy. Include a contact email address. Finally, also request that a Nebula Awards Commissioner post links to the review files in their Forum.

*British Fantasy Awards*: Form and info to submit ideas for the Fantasy award: http://www.britishfantasysociety.org/british-fantasy-awards/the-british-fantasy-awards-a-short-history/

*Readers Favorite Reviews:* Free review copy: submit files via a form at: https://readersfavorite.com/book-reviews.htm

*National Book Critics Award*: Email the organizers to suggest your title for nomination. Most of these critics are also in charge of reviewing books for the top review publications, so when you send your book to them you're shooting two rabbits with one stone.

**Other Types of Contacts to Research:**
Alumni magazines for your colleges
Contact faculty in the relevant field for course adoptions
Send blurb requests to best-selling or award-winning writers
Radio and TV stations, newspapers and other media in the region

# CREATING A YOUTUBE BOOK TRAILER

If you want to add a dynamic element to your website, or if you'd like to create a video advertisement to post on other websites, the easiest book trailer creation program that I found is YouTube's Creator Studio. You can log into this program through your Google+ or Gmail account, or you can create a new account, if you don't have one of these. Using this tool is free, and you can also use it to create animatics or short animated cartoons with audio.

From Creator Studio, click on the "Create" tab and choose "Video Editor". Here are the icons you'll see at the top that you can use to edit the trailer:

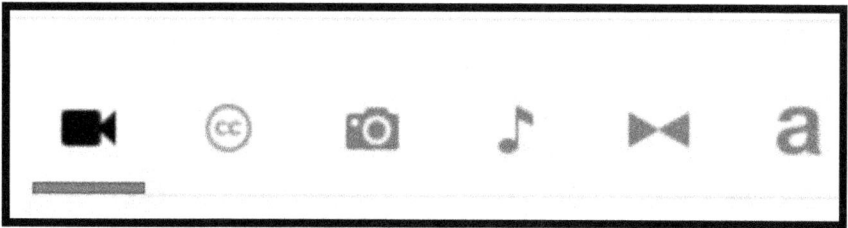

**Fig. 9.1. YouTube Video Editor Tools**

The first icon lets you edit together video segments, or insert video segments together with photos and other content. The third image of a camera allows you to insert photos into the trailer that hold for a standard 5 seconds (more or less). These photos can be any images in various formats, which can include your cover image, or photos or paintings that explain the content of your book. You can also create pages with text and backgrounds in InDesign that you can convert into a .pdf via an export, and then into a .jpeg in Photoshop. If you've seen book trailers on GoodReads with backgrounds, cover images and descriptive text, this is in part how those are done. You can also do a simple Word document with the text you want to insert, and then convert it into a .pdf, and then into a .jpeg. You might want to have a slide with a photo and then a slide with text, or you can merge these two on the same slides. The fourth icon with the note is used to insert music over the videos or images in the book trailer. When you click on it, you'll have an option to insert any of the free public domain music available via YouTube, or to import your own music files.

Once you click on the icon you need, you'll be able to upload images or find and select music, videos or images that you want to use. Then you will drag the various pieces you want to utilize into the "Drag Video Here" and "Drag Audio Here" lines under the black screen that represents the video you are putting together. When everything is in the desired order, you'll click on "Publish" and in a few hours the trailer will be up on your YouTube channel.

There are several ways to share this trailer with your fans. Under each of your videos, you'll see options to "Share", "Embed" or "Email" the video. To "Share" the video, you're given a URL link that you can post online or send out for fans to click on. The "Share" tab also allows you to post a note on various social media platforms with a link to the video. You will need the "Embed" option for websites that allow you to embed a video on a page, which means that it will appear like a tiny video screen on the page and will be frozen on a key image. This way, fans coming to a website will not only see the text of a link, but will see a video screen that they can activate by clicking on it. If you have a free WordPress website, you can embed a YouTube video by clicking on "Add Media", then "Insert from URL" and then typing the "Share" URL link for the video. You would have to have a paid WordPress account to insert the video directly from YouTube or by pasting the "Embed" html text provided by YouTube's Video Creator.

In 2015-6, I experimented with a few other types of book trailers. I especially liked working with Movie Studio 13 to combine bits of film and to edit sound, film and effects together. I also tried using the Natural Readers text-to-speech program to create different accents for a video without needing voice actors. These experiments are available on my YouTube channel. I don't know if they are that much better than a simple YouTube combination of images and public domain music. If you want to make a quick trailer for a GoodReads board or to share with friends, I wouldn't invest money into these options. I'm sure that if I spent a bit more on high-end video software, I would come up with better results. One of my better attempts was with Flash animation, which is a part of the CS6 Suite; and this is a costlier option in comparison with Movie Studio (which is intended for home rather than commercial applications).

# CONCLUSION

In conclusion, there are many programs a potential publisher has to learn to produce books in today's marketplace. Access to the publishing industry is looser today than it was a hundred years ago, but only if you sift through the various manuals and learn the tools that are necessary to perfect the publishing craft. Specializing in editing, design or marketing, rather than trying to do all three parts of the job should lower the quantity of programs you have to learn and should make the job manageable. Therefore, a growing publishing house needs interns and assistants to help lighten the Editor-in-Chief's load, or all sides of the production process suffer in the rush (unless of course the Editor can juggle all of the balls on their own).

*If you are that Editor/Publisher who is reading this book hoping to start a press on their own*, I wish you lots of hard work!

*To my Anaphora interns*: Thank you for your help, it is most appreciated. Please let me know if you notice any mistakes in this *Guide* and I will do my best to correct them.

*The End*

# OTHER
# ANAPHORA LITERARY
# PRESS TITLES

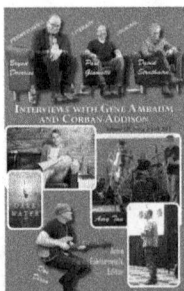

*PLJ: Interviews with Gene Ambaum and Corban Addison: VII:3, Fall 2015*
**Editor: Anna Faktorovich**

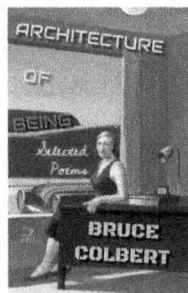

*Architecture of Being*
**By: Bruce Colbert**

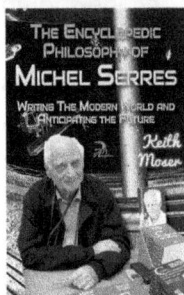

*The Encyclopedic Philosophy of Michel Serres*
**By: Keith Moser**

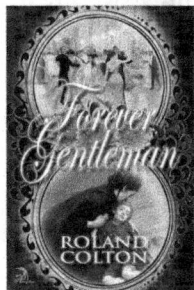

*Forever Gentleman*
**By: Roland Colton**

*Janet Yellen*
**By: Marie Bussing-Burks**

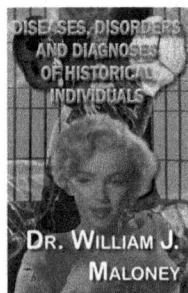

*Diseases, Disorders, and Diagnoses of Historical Individuals*
**By: William J. Maloney**

*Armageddon at Maidan*
**By: Vasyl Baziv**

*Vovochka*
**By: Alexander J. Motyl**

www.ingramcontent.com/pod-product-compliance
Lightning Source LLC
Chambersburg PA
CBHW060506280326
41933CB00014B/2881